A Legacy
of Champions

The Story of the Men Who Built
University of Kentucky Basketball

Written by
Rick Bozich, Pat Forde, C. Ray Hall and Mark Woods

Edited by
Mike Bynum

SPORTS

Research Assistance: Sharon Bidwell, Bill Ellison, Harry Bryan and the staff of *The Courier-Journal*; Brooks Downing and the University of Kentucky Sports Information Office; the University of Kentucky Archives; and David Coyle.

ISBN 1-57028-169-6
ISBN (leatherbound) 1-57028-179-3

Cover and Book Design by Chris Kozlowski, Detroit.

Published by:
Masters Press
2647 Waterfront Parkway East Drive
Indianapolis, IN 46214

Contents

A
Special
Bond

By Pat Forde

I
t's been said *ad infinitum* that being a basketball fan in Kentucky is a lifelong occupation.

Now we know that's incorrect.

It's longer than that.

Why wait to start at birth? A few years ago one Kentucky Wildcats fan mailed an ultrasound of his unborn baby to coach Rick Pitino, for storage in his future recruiting files.

And why bother to stop at death? In 1991, a man from Pikeville was buried with a card from mountain hero John Pelphrey and his Unforgettable teammates in his casket, toting the Cats with him into the Hereafter. The man was such a UK fan that even after being diagnosed with terminal cancer, he wouldn't take his morphine on game days. Made him too drowsy to concentrate on Cawood's flowing words.

Of course, it's in the period between birth and death that basketball fully seizes the souls of the citizenry, like nothing else can.

In 1913-14, the Wildcats won 12 games and lost 2.

The World Book Encyclopedia's section on Kentucky contains a wealth of information on thoroughbred racing and not a syllable on basketball. But the Kentucky Derby lasts two minutes, and often is won by inordinately wealthy outsiders or bluebloods the common man can't relate to.

As anyone who lives here can tell you, basketball is the true love of the people.

From birth to death (or longer), the allegiance to the game and its teams is handed down from parents to children and carried on. Kentucky is among the nation's leaders in percentage of residents who are natives of the state. One dynamic of that is the cultural and

Dave Lawrence, an all-American forward in 1935.

social continuity of basketball, our old standby.

When all else fails, basketball gives the old and young — the poor and the rich, the black and the white, the city and the country — something to talk about.

Despite the frequency and intensity of hoop-related arguments in our state, basketball is, as much as anything else, our common ground.

That's why the rhythmic slapping of ball on polished wood might as well be the official state sound of Kentucky.

Or ball on beaten earth, as a boy on the side of a mountain in Manchester learns to shoot at a goal attached to a telephone pole.

Or ball on concrete, as kids in Louisville's West End play on a bent rim at a public-housing playground.

Basketball is an up-from-the-boot-straps game. And in Kentucky, where difficult circumstance is spread across racial and geographical lines, those stories can be found all over the state.

Kids from the Western Coal Field and Purchase regions emulate Travis Ford, the tiny point guard who drove

The 1914-15 Wildcats posted a record of 7 wins and 5 losses.

UK to the 1993 Final Four and has since moved on to author a book, star in a movie and become the basketball coach at Campbellsville College.

Kids from Northern Kentucky can hear about Dave Cowens, the fiery red-head from Newport who got away to Florida State, then matriculated to the Boston Celtics and the NBA Hall of Fame.

Kids from Louisville know Darrell Griffith as a living legend, the sky-walker who brought the first NCAA title home to the Cardinals.

Kids in Appalachia know all about Richie Farmer, perhaps the archetypical hero of the Little Guy. And Pelphrey. And before them Wah Wah Jones and Johnny Cox and many others.

And in the Pennyroyal Region they are celebrating the youngster who may be UK's next small-town star, J.P. Blevins, the pride of Edmonton County.

All these diverse areas, joined at the sound of the bouncing ball.

It is the balm that medicates a beaten-down psyche. It is the pride that suffuses divergent peoples in divergent

Ermal Allen was a two-sport star — in football and basketball — for Kentucky.

Lee Huber, a two-time all-American guard in 1940 and 1941.

locales. It is the most visible and visceral payback for decades of scorn, pity and apathy from the rest of America.

Outsiders can strip-mine the mountains, propagate the hillbilly stereotypes and generally yawn in our direction. But just try to beat us in basketball.

Ball on wood is joy to the ears that

have so often heard sorrow.

Amid all the glum stats about where Kentucky ranks in economy, education and health, there are the glowing stats about where it ranks on the hardwood.

You look around the commonwealth

for superlatives, and it's hard to find many — except in basketball.

There are UK's 129 consecutive homecourt wins. Rupp's 876 victories. Diddle's 759. Crum's 613. There are Rupp's four national titles, Crum's two, Hall's one and Pitino's one. Nineteen Final Four appearances from the Cats, Cardinals and Hilltoppers combined.

There was the Fabulous Five. The Fiddlin' Five. Rupp's Runts. The Doctors of Dunk. The Unforgettables. The Untouchables.

There have been dozens of all-Americans. Scores of memorable victories. Hundreds of thousands of fans who can declare "We are the best," even if the citizens of Indiana and North Carolina can give them an argument.

And beneath the abiding loyalties to our college teams, on a level even closer to Kentucky's roots, there is the bedrock support of high school basketball.

There are packed gyms from the Mississippi River flood plain to the jagged hills around Harlan. There is a rich folklore that celebrates the triumphs of the Little Guys — Inez, Hazel Green, Hindman, Brewers, Cuba, Edmonson County, Clay County, Breckinridge County, Paintsville.

Such folklore befits a state that perceives itself a Little Guy in the nation's eyes.

Back before the state improved its road structure and began consolidating schools, almost every town had its own high school. These were the anchors of small communities — and at one time, more than 600 high schools played varsity basketball (that number is now less than 300).

The good people of Oddville, Lone Jack or Sinking Fork might never have dreamed of getting to see the Cats in person, but they could sure get into the gym down the road to see their local boys play.

And the local boys weren't playing for some Class C title; they were playing to win the Sweet Sixteen and rule over all of Kentucky. In the commonwealth it was, is, and hopefully forever will be One Class, One Champion. Those triumphs of the Little Guys over the Big City Schools is what makes the mythology of the Sweet Sixteen so outsized — and now that Indiana has killed its single-class tournament, Kentucky can stand alone as owner of the purest prep basketball in all the land.

Where ball meets wood is where we look the rest of America in the eye.

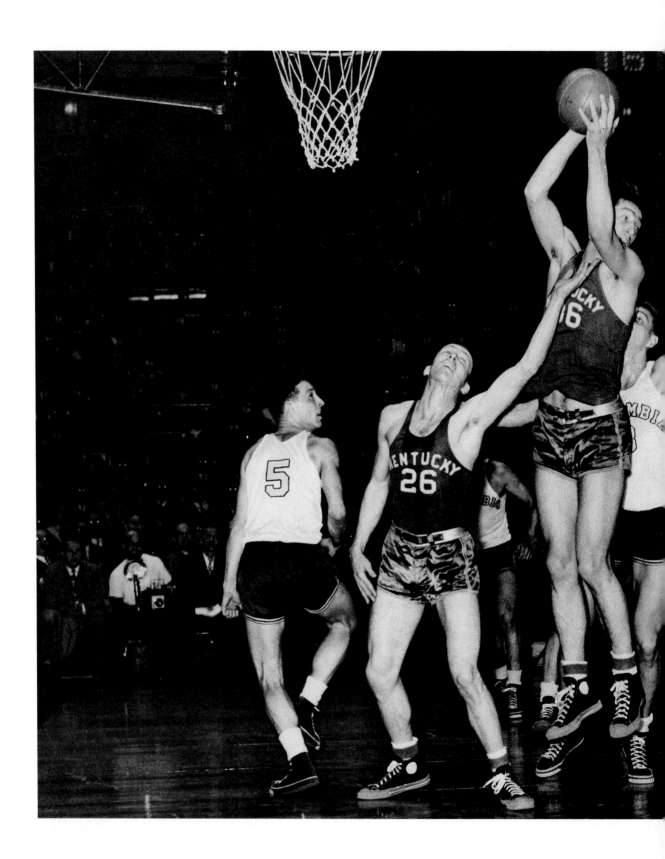

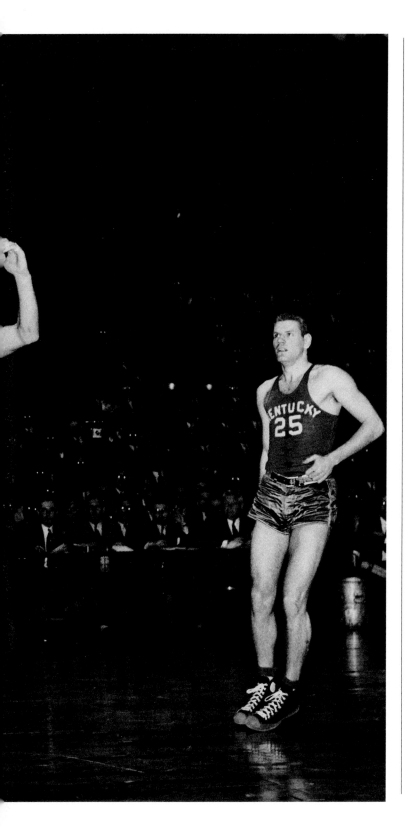

Alex Groza (36) grabs a rebound against Columbia in the 1948 NCAA Tournament.

O f course, that hasn't always been the case. From roughly the turn of the century on, Kentuckians have been straining under the yoke of a bad national image.

To the nation, this was the state that assassinated its governor, William Goebel, in 1900, then nearly dissolved into civil war. The state of feuding hill-billies. The state of the Black Patch War, wherein tobacco farmers took up

Alex Groza, a three-time all-American center in 1947, 1948 and 1949.

In the Spring of 1949, Rupp announced to a UK Alumni Association banquet that the Fabulous Five's jerseys would be retired.

arms against a tobacco-firm monopoly.

In Cherokee dialect, Kentucky is said to mean "the dark and bloody ground." The state was doing its best to live down to that billing.

But by 1920, the game invented decades earlier by Dr. James Naismith in Springfield, Mass., was being polished to a pretty fine sheen in Kentucky. Captained by Basil Hayden,

After the 1948 NCAA Tournament in New York City, a large crowd awaited the Wildcats' return to Lexington.

Kentucky's first all-American, the 1920-21 Wildcats went 13-1 and won the Southern Intercollegiate Althetic Association (predecessor of the Southeastern Conference) tournament by whipping Tulane, Mercer, Mississippi A&M and Georgia.

UK went on to record winning seasons in seven of the next nine years. And in 1928, high school teams from

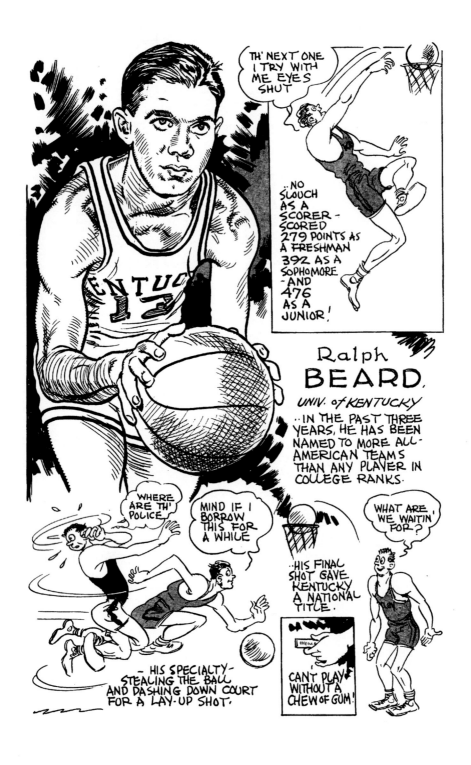

Adolph Rupp's Wildcats were among the first college teams on television. Their first tv game was against St. John's in 1951.

Ashland and tiny Carr Creek went to a national tournament in Chicago. Ash-

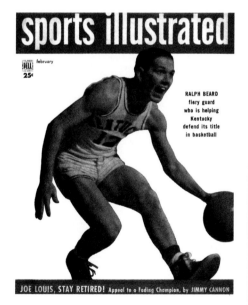

Ralph Beard appeared on the cover of the original Sports Illustrated in February 1949.

land won the hardware and Carr Creek won the hearts.

Then, in 1930, a Kansan who had coached high-school ball in Illinois came to Lexington to coach the Cats.

His name was Adolph Rupp.

By his third season Kentucky was champion of the Southeastern Conference. By the mid-1930's UK annually ruled the league and the region. By the 1940's UK was winning national titles, Olympic gold medals and playing before record crowds at Madison Square Garden. Rupp was recruiting nationally and locally, winning big with kids from the big cities and the hills of Eastern Kentucky, and he cemented

Bill Spivey, who stood 7 feet tall, dominated opposing teams and earned a legendary reputation of epic proportions.

the bond between the mountain folk and the Cats with his quote from the Bible:

"I lift up mine eyes to the hills, whence cometh my help."

Here was a man — a hero — courting the scorned. Here he was, offering his champions up to the dispossessed. The fans devoured it all: the winning, the entertaining style of play, the Man in the Brown Suit.

Here, at long last, was something Kentuckians could thump their chests over.

They built a 11,000-seat pantheon to Rupp in 1950, Memorial Coliseum.

Kentucky vs *Ga. Tech*
MEMORIAL COLISEUM
Saturday, January 8, 1955 — 8:00 p.m.

OFFICIAL PROGRAM—10 CENTS

The Cats lost to Georgia Tech, 59-58 — one of 3 losses that season.

Outside the commonwealth, people laughed at a gym that size. No way they'd ever fill that thing.

They did. And UK proceeded to become virtually unbeatable in the building.

That was the Kentucky we wanted the outside world to see. While then-attorney general Bobby Kennedy was opening America's eyes to the conditions in Appalachia, UK was still winning games. While mining disasters and Black Lung were killing Kentuckians, UK was still winning games.

Until John Wooden planted his sceptre in the ground on the West Coast, there was nothing in the history of college basketball to compare to Kentucky.

Ultimately, of course, Kentuckians had their glory besmirched. After a point-shaving scandal and NCAA rules violations UK's program was shut down in 1952-53, the height of Rupp's glory years. And it might have been at that time that one of the less laudable characteristics of the Cat basketball fan manifested itself:

The bunker mentality. The belief that people Outside, jealous of our success, are out to get us.

At various times there have been various blames. The media is out to get us. The NCAA is out to get us. UCLA is out to get us. The refs are out to get us. The Eastern elite, who already look down on us and strip-mine our land, are out to get us.

Things are interesting in the bunker.

UK fans are loyal, cheerful, honest, trustworthy. ... They will fill 2,000 seats in a 2,400-seat gym in Maui, leaving seven other schools to fill the rest. They will fill 20,000 seats in Rupp Arena during a blizzard to see a routine rout of a bad opponent. They will provide The UK Wakeup Call at hotels during tournament time, as shouts of "Bluuuuuuue! Whiiiiiiite!" ring through the lobby shortly after dawn.

But life in the bunker also can be both grandiose and petty at the same time.

Grandiosity: When Pitino took the UK basketball team to Italy in the summer of 1995, a group of Cat fans went along. Of course. One day the group was touring a coliseum in Verona that predated the Roman Colosseum.

Governor Happy Chandler visits with the Fiddlin' Five in 1958.

Rupp and his Runts finished second in the 1966 NCAA Tournament.

The tour guide mentioned that the coliseum seated more than 20,000 people. A member of the group murmured, "Hell, our arena's bigger than that."

Pettiness: The absurd hullaballoo in 1996 over UK's denim uniforms. Pitino was bombarded with complaints that the uniforms weren't "true Kentucky blue," and, in fact, were closer to the satanic sky blue worn by hated North Carolina.

So as the Cats have bounced between triumph and shame over the decades since, that attitude has remained in tow. But in what might be an example of grace and perspective attained through the remarkable resurrection

Rupp's Runts at a movie theatre in Tuscaloosa, Ala., in 1966.

after the last scandal, UK fans have come to regard a loss as one of their favorite games of all time: the 104-103 overtime classic against Duke in 1992.

Maybe, along with all the victories

Joe B. Hall's 1977-78 Wildcats were national champs with a 30-2 record.

and the fun, that can be part of Rick Pitino's legacy at Kentucky: leading (some) fans out of the bunker.

populace something to put on a pedestal.

The astonishing emotional out-pouring that accompanied the death of Princess Diana tells us that people still have a thing for royalty. They like having someone or something to leave them awestruck, to bow down before.

Here in Kentucky, basketball players are our royalty.

Enter the player. Hear the voices drop to a whisper. See the fingers furtively point.

Is that (fill in the blank with Derek Anderson, Kenny Walker or Cliff Hagan)? Yes!

If you've been to a small-town gym where the Cats have entered to screams and wails, you understand. If you've been out on the town in Louisville and seen the procession of hand-shakers and autograph-seekers approaching the Cardinals, you understand. If you've seen Rick Pitino try in vain to eat din-ner for five minutes without interrup-tion, you understand.

And if UK's players and coaches are royalty, Rupp Arena is Buckingham Palace. And just about as hard to get into.

Everybody can see the changing of the guard in front of the palace, but few

I f basketball in Kentucky is a vehicle for raising a friendly-but-fragile populace to the level of others, it also contains a paradox.

Basketball in Kentucky gives the

get *past* the guards.

Same with Rupp: Everyone can mill around in the Lexington Civic Center before a game, drink some bourbon and predict a Cat blowout. But not everyone gets through the doors to see the action in person.

Tickets are impossible, the remoteness adding to the mythology of the program. Death and divorce have produced bitter family squabbles over the rights to the ducats. One woman on the aforementioned Italy trip went overseas to see her Cats but had never seen them play in Rupp.

Which in part explains the royal status conferred on the people's emissary, Cawood Ledford. In addition to being near-flawless with his call of a game, he *was* UK fans' keys to the mythical kingdom. Especially in the days before most games were televised.

You hear a lot these days in Kentucky about the diminished coal industry, the challenged tobacco industry, the threatened thoroughbred industry — but the hoop is as good as ever.

Adolph Rupp won 4 national championships with a 876-190 record in 42 seasons.

In fact, ball on wood might never have sounded better than in 1996. Kentucky won the national title. Northern Kentucky won the Division II title. Sullivan College won the national junior college title. And another chapter of charming mountain mythology was added to the Sweet Sixteen when Paintsville, pride of Appalachia, won that title.

So you can understand why the passions just may run deeper for the roundball sport than for anything else in the commonwealth. That may not speak well for the societal priorities, but I believe it speaks the truth.

Maybe we should all pay more attention to politics. But then again, the politicians are right there alongside us watching the games.

The late Gov. Happy Chandler counted himself one of Adolph Rupp's best friends and used to sing *My Old Kentucky Home* on Senior Day. Former Gov. Wallace Wilkinson allied himself with Eddie Sutton and against school president David Roselle when the deal went sour at UK in the late 1980's. And state legislators count comp lower-level tickets at Rupp Arena among their most cherished perks.

In fact, wearing a UK basketball jer-

Dan Issel, Kentucky's explosive center, who was named all-American in 1969 and 1970, scored 29 points to lead the Wildcats to a 115-85 win over Kansas in 1969.

sey isn't a half bad launching pad for a political career. U.S. Rep. Scotty Baesler is a former guard for Rupp, and

Joe B. Hall succeded his mentor, Rupp, and posted a 297-100 record in 13 seasons.

you *know* Richie Farmer would be a lock to represent his mountain district if he should ever run for office.

But as important as basketball is to the kings, it is even more vital to the commoners. They love the Cats at Idle

Richie Farmer and former heavyweight champ Muhammad Ali clown for the photographers at a Kentucky game in 1992.

Hour Country Club in Lexington, but they *need* the Cats in the hollers and small towns and remote areas of the state.

Whenever I'm asked to describe Kentucky basketball fans, my mind immediately tracks back 10 years to a story former Courier-Journal writer Scott Fowler turned in from Jeff, Ky., a dot-on-the-map town in Perry County.

The occasion was a preseason UK scrimmage, back in the days when the NCAA condoned statewide tub-thumping exhibitions. About 3,000

fans squeezed into Dilce Combs High School's 2,000-seat gym to see the Cats.

At halftime the game ball, autographed by UK coach Eddie Sutton, was auctioned off for $1,450 to a man named Ted Cook, a tire dealer from London, Ky. His explanation?

"I ain't got no sense when it comes to

Jared Prickett was selected to the NCAA All-Southeast Regional Team after he scored 22 points, had 10 rebounds and 5 assists against Florida State as a freshman in 1993.

basketball," Cook said, unwittingly speaking for an entire state.

Wally Clark ain't got no sense. He's the fellow who pulls his Ford Fiesta camper in front of Memorial Coliseum every year to get the jump on being the first man through the doors at Midnight Madness. Last year Ol' Wally was there for *38 days,* which should have been ample time for the psych department to send someone across campus and help the guy.

Bob Wiggins ain't got no sense. Although he does have a lot of money. Bob attended 615 consecutive UK basketball games, all over this occasionally great land of ours.

Bill Keightley ain't got no sense. He's been washing jocks and socks as the UK equipment manager for 35 years, dating back to the Rupp years. As a True Blue Believer, Keightley carries no small animosity for the Cats' archrival Louisville Cardinals. When Louisville radio network color man Jock Sutherland once paid a visit to a UK press conference, Keightley hid around a corner and refused to come out until Sutherland was gone.

And then there is Hazel Porter. If you want to know about Kentucky basketball fans who ain't got no sense, you need to know about Hazel.

"This is Kentucky *Wildcat* country *purrsonified,*" Hazel's 81-year-old voice croons on her answering machine. "I'm out helping Tubby (Smith) and Hal (Mumme) recruit, so leave a message if you want me to call you back. *Go,* Cats! This is the fight song (whereupon an electronic warble of the UK fight song plays)..."

Hazel lives in Frankfort and works for state government. In Hazel's hierarchy of powers, there is God, there is the Democratic party and there are the Cats. And not necessarily in that order on game day.

One of the prominent features of Hazel's house is an autographed picture of Pitino, sent to her on the occasion of her 75th birthday. She once took snapshots of Pitino *on television* because she figured the end of his tenure at UK was coming near (she was right). She once threw a pie at a sports writer who had written something about the Cats that she didn't like.

When Hazel got her tickets to the 1996 Final Four, she sat in her car and

Jamal Mashburn, a 1993 all-American, reaches for a layup against Michigan's Juwan Howard in their 1993 Final Four game.

In his seventh season at the helm of the Wildcats, won their sixth national title, by defeating Syracuse, 76-67, in the Final game of the 1996 NCAA Tournament.

Right: Reggie Hanson scored 11 points against Auburn in March 1991 in the Wildcats' final game under NCAA sanctions.

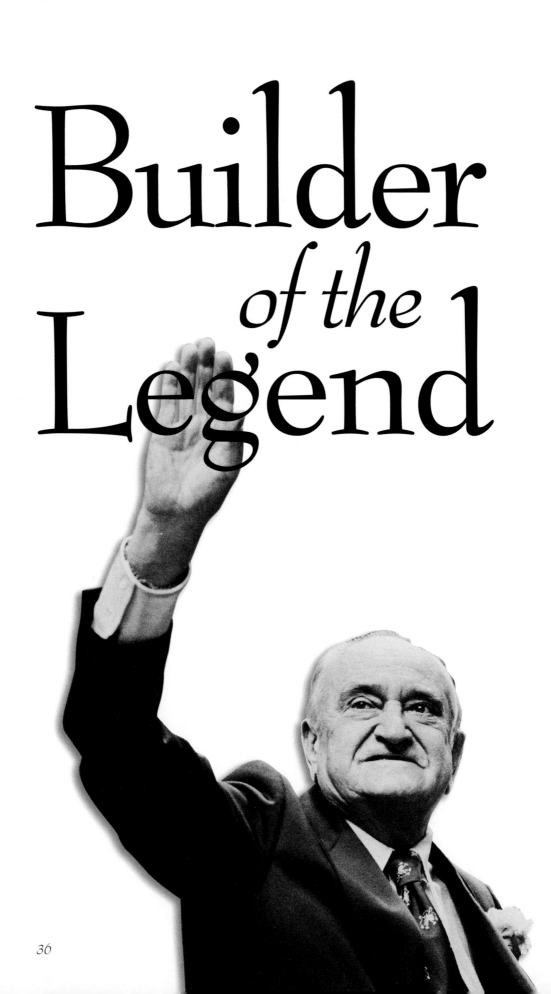

Builder
of the
Legend

By C. Ray Hall

Rupp.

Like "love" and "hate," it's a four-letter word.

In 42 years as University of Kentucky basketball coach, Adolph Rupp incited love, hate and practically every other emotion a heart can hold.

Two decades after his death, he can still stir up passions. To some, he was the spiritual savior of a downtrodden state. To others, Rupp was the devil in the deep blue sea. Then and now, he transcends the game. Like many icons, he is best explained in terms of other icons.

"He was a Patton on the basketball floor," says Dick Parsons, who played and coached for Rupp. "If you remember George C. Scott from the opening of the movie, *Patton*, that was coach Rupp."

The comparison is double-edged. Like Patton, Rupp was a flinty, laser-eyed master of profanity-laced persuasion. Like Scott, he was a consummate actor.

"Sometimes," Parsons says, "he would give the damnedest pre-game talk, and the kids would be so intense, ready to knock that door down. He'd kind of grin and say, 'How do you like that?' He could perform. He could act mad even if he wasn't. He was a master."

Like all actors, Rupp really wanted to direct. Around him, you were never quite sure whether he was acting or directing (and offering witty asides to an unseen audience that, like him, was in on the joke, whereas you were not).

KENTUCKY

HANK LUISETTI DIAGRAM BOARD

He was not only an iconic presence, but an ironic one: He could be in the action and above it.

"There was never anyone really close to him," says Parsons, a UK fund-raiser. "Even when you were around him a lot, you were not quite sure you understood him. His personality was quite unique. There was never a clone of Coach Rupp."

Adolph Frederick Rupp was round of face and body, but lean and angular of thought, and brutally direct of expression. He was sharp of tongue, short of temper, long of memory, and large of ego. He had little use for fools, jesters, moral lapsers, or free-thinkers.

He made allowances, though, for the sublimely talented. From 1962-64, Cotton Nash was a bigger star than Rupp. A *Sport* magazine writer proclaimed him the most handsome athlete he had ever seen. As a senior, Nash averaged 24 points a game, tying Cliff Hagan's season record. Six years later, Dan Issel averaged 33.9.

Rupp's reaction: "I'm kind of sorry you broke Cliff's record, but I'm glad you broke that s.o.b. Nash's record,"

Rupp diagrams his offense for the Cats' 1948 NCAA Tournament.

Issel recalls in his biography, *Parting Shots*.

"He didn't like Nash," Issel wrote, "because Nash was his own man."

Rupp wouldn't tolerate slouchers: the sight of a player idling about with a toothpick dangling from his mouth made him dyspeptic. If slouchers provoked him so, imagine his wrath toward slackers. Practices went full-speed, and were usually harder than games.

"Coach Rupp knew how to sharpen iron with iron," says Jim Dinwiddie, a Leitchfield, Ky., lawyer who played on some of his last teams (1969-71).

Parsons theorizes that Rupp's spirit was forged on the unforgiving Kansas plains, where his father died when he was 9. "On that farm when he was a young kid ... he knew what hardships were. He made that comment occasionally, about being on the farm and how tough it was."

The man with the iron will was surprisingly soft on the outside. People took stock of his large hands, then noted how soft they were. Late in life, those hands had a doughy quality — white and soft, almost as if they could be kneaded. Something in his eyes and his thin scrawl of a smile made you think he knew more than he was letting on. Which was something, because he let on that he knew about everything worth knowing. Among the words to describe Rupp, "self-effacing" may be the last to come to mind.

"He set records for vanity that will never be broken," Dave Kindred wrote in his book *Basketball: The Dream Game in Kentucky.*

(It should be noted that Kindred wrote those words long before Rick Pitino ascended to Rupp's throne.)

Rupp was a man of appetites — chili and bourbon for the flesh, fame and glory for the spirit. When players showed up for school, he reminded them to be on time, go to class, work hard "and be damn sure you go to church on Sunday." Rupp may have showed his players the path to salvation, but he was doomed — to the impossible pursuit of perfection.

"He never was totally, totally satisfied," says Ralph Beard (1946-49). "We beat Vanderbilt in the first round of the SEC Tournament one time, 98-29, and he still wasn't satisfied, so you knew then that it never would happen. He never afforded anybody that luxury, including himself, in the four years I was with him."

Beard and his "Fabulous Five" team-

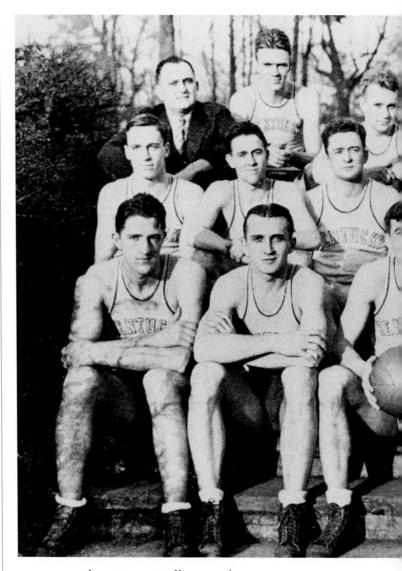

mates — Alex Groza, Wallace "Wah Wah" Jones, Kenny Rollins and Cliff Barker, won the 1948 NCAA title. The next season, they returned nearly intact — with Dale Barnstable instead of Rollins — to repeat, amassing a two-year record of 68-5.

In between, the Fabulous Five formed part of the 14-player 1948

The 1930-31 Wildcats — Rupp's first team — won 15 games and lost 3.

Olympic team. In those days, a tournament determined the Olympic representatives. The NIT champ, St. Louis, sat out the affair, citing a loss of class time (a prospect Kentucky apparently found less troubling). In the final,

Kentucky, faced the AAU champ, Phillips Oilers.

"Cliff Barker broke his nose and they beat us 53-49," Beard recalls. "The winning team provided the head Olympic coach. The losing team, which was us, provided the assistant. The first thing he said to us was, 'I want to thank you sons of bitches for making me an assistant coach for the first time in my career.'"

No one laughed.

"Even though he was going to the Olympics, getting a gold medal, by God, he wanted to be the head coach," Beard says. "That's one of the things I learned from him. He would not accept defeat, and he didn't want anybody that played for him to accept defeat. And it always killed him, as it did us."

(Footnote in history: Rupp assisted one Omar Browning. In the title game, France fell, 65-21.)

In later years, Rupp had softened. Watching his boys draped in gold medals at London's Wembley Stadium was one of his proudest moments, he said.

Rupp prospered in a basketball era so unlike the present as to seem imaginary. Recruiting? Prospects came to him. In the 1940's, he and his equally stern assistant, flat-topped Harry Lancaster, supervised tryouts that attracted more than 100 players, aching for the few scholarships. Alumni Gym, a 2,800-seat red brick structure dating to 1924, couldn't accommodate even the students, whose tickets were rationed; a student got to see every third game. Scouting was superficial, compared to today. Television was still a dream. Players's observations did not decorate newspaper stories. The mystery added to the mystique. UK basketball had one voice, and it was Rupp's.

He had an orotund speaking style, inflating and stretching vowels. He called his players "the booyys," making the word rise in the middle. He began his observations with, "Waayuull" so that every statement sounded like a pronouncement.

It made him a media favorite, though it's unlikely he would have abided today's saturation coverage. Near the end of his career, the team was working out the afternoon before a night game. A TV crew bustled about, setting up its equipment. Rupp bade a manager to banish the intruders.

Rupp and Alex Groza inspect the length of a hotel bed while on a road trip.

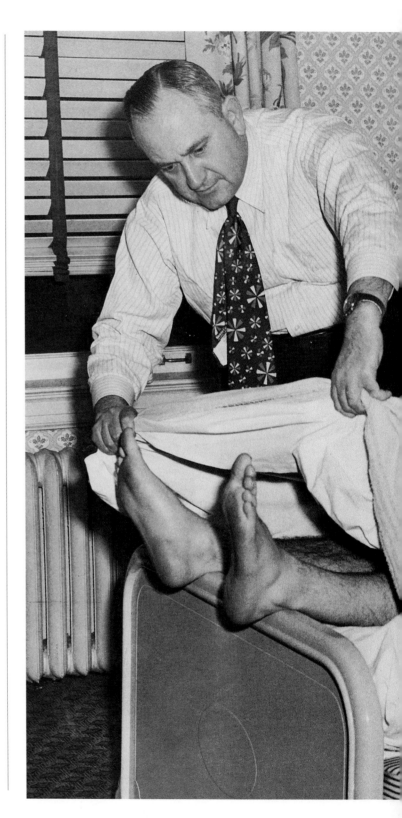

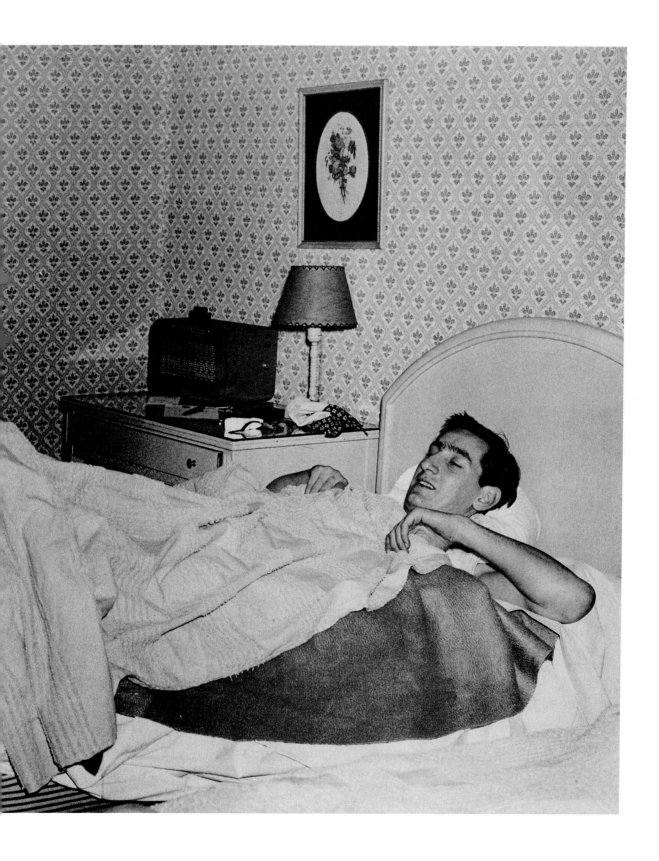

"It became clear that diplomatic gestures were futile," Dinwiddie says. "A quick decision was made ... to prepare an offense for a full-court press, with instructions to bomb the hell out of the cameras at midcourt, with apparent passes.

"After a few well-executed missed catches," Dinwiddie says, the TV folks retreated.

Rupp abided no intrusions on practice, even by insiders. "The thing I still remember is how quiet the practices were," says Larry Conley, the broadcaster who was a 6-foot-3 forward on the famous 1966 team, Rupp's Runts.

"All you ever heard was the bounce of the ball," says Parsons (1959-61). "Coach Rupp called it his classroom. He wanted total concentration."

"It was like you were in a vacuum" Beard says. "Nobody said anything."

One day, a sharp-shooter from Ohio named Jim Line found out just how sacred the silence was.

"There was Coach Rupp down at one end in his starched khakis — there was Coach Lancaster at the other end in his starched khakis," Beard recalls.

Rupp and his longtime assistant, Harry Lancaster.

"We always had a 30-minute shooting drill. There wasn't anything but the screech of the shoes, and the basketballs pounding."

Until the day Jim Line started whistling.

"Coach Rupp came up like a dog on a point," Beard recalls, "and he said, 'Harry, who in the hell is doing that whistling out there?' Says, 'By God if he wants to sing we'll send him over to the music Guignol [the student fine-arts theater]. Out here we play basketball.'

Sarcasm was only one of Rupp's weapons. The others included showmanship, superstition, Scripture (occasionally), stubbornness, and a supreme self-confidence. He gave A's to all the students in his basketball-coaching class, on the theory that anyone who learned the game from him deserved nothing less. One of the quotes often attributed to him is: "Keep 'em close, boys, and I'll think of something."

After scouting an opponent, Parsons once advised Rupp, "Maybe we ought to work on the press."

"Why?" Rupp asked. "We're not going to be behind."

In the 1960's, he relented and began playing a zone defense. This flew in the face of his historic reliance on man-to-man, and its attendant emphasis on personal accountability. When reporters asked about the zone, he replied, "That was no zone. That was a stratified transitional hyperbolic paraboloid with a man between the ball and the basket."

Once, you could simply rely on the numbers to tell the Rupp story. He coached four national champions, 27 Southeastern Conference champs, 10 consensus first-team all-Americans and three Hall of Famers — Issel, Hagan and Frank Ramsey. (Pat Riley, '67, likely will be the fourth.) For 18 years, Rupp held the record for most NCAA basketball championships — until he was spectacularly deposed by UCLA's John Wooden. For 25 years, Rupp owned the record for most victories, 876. North Carolina's Dean Smith passed him last spring. Soon, Smith stepped down at age 66. At 70, Rupp was still trying vainly to keep going — to coach as long as he breathed.

Rupp coached his last game in 1972 (a 73-54 loss to Florida State). With every new season, he recedes in the record books. Every new coach of the decade pushes him a little more toward antiquity, in the shadow land of Hank Iba, Clair Bee and Ed Diddle. A television generation assured of the genius of Jim Boeheim and Tom Penders probably could not tell Adolph Rupp from Adolphe Menjou. ("Fame," as George C. Scott-Patton said in the movie, "is fleeting.")

Even in Kentucky, there are folks who would declare Rupp a relic best forgotten, overshadowed in the Enlightenment of the Rick Pitino era. Perhaps a Biblical metaphor is more apt: To some UK fans, Rupp-Pitino is Old Testament God vs. New Testament God — wrath vs. redemption.

But Rupp is always there, as distant as the sky and almost as big, as deep as the 23,500-seat arena that bears his name. Kentucky remains the winningest team in college basketball history. Rupp's handprints cover more than half those victories, and will until Kentucky scores No. 1,753, probably in the next millennium. Rupp's imprint is on four of UK's six NCAA championships — five, if you count Joe Hall, coach of the 1978 champs, as part of his lineage.

Rupp's shadow falls on Pitino and the sixth title, too: UK athletics director C.M. Newton hired Pitino 38 years after playing for Rupp's 1951 champs.

Rupp, the emperor of what *Sports Illustrated* called "the Roman Empire of college basketball," made Pitino possible — or necessary.

Pitino, recently departed for the the Roman Empire of pro basketball — the Boston Celtics — remains sharply etched in Kentuckians' memory. The same was true of Rupp. But as time goes by, the Man in the Brown Suit — so called because of his game-night wardrobe — has become the Man in the Blue Mist, a mystery wrapped in a mystique.

He was the most brilliant basketball coach of this or any other time. Or he was the lucky beneficiary of Southern hospitality, scoring most of his victories against schools that took basketball about as seriously as badminton. (He once beat Georgia by 77. His players grabbed a surreal 108 rebounds against Ole Miss, a team that went 0-36, against Rupp.) One coaching rival, Johnny Dee, likened Rupp's rule of the South to hauling a hockey team to Texas and taking on all comers.

He was a charming, disarming man. Or he was a cantankerous old coot. In his autobiography, *Parting Shots*, Issel

wrote: "Coach Rupp could be mean, but not mean-spirited. It's just that he was very disciplined. Most coaches kick you in the butt one minute and pat you on the back the next; Rupp just kicked you in the butt all the time."

He was the most notorious tightwad this side of Jack Benny. Or he was a generous man, so full of charity and bonhommie he willingly subdued his usually regal persona beneath a Shriner's fez to raise money for good works.

He was so profane he could have blistered Bobby Knight and Pitino in a cursing contest, one-on-two. Or he rationed his cursing, solely for emphasis, and it is memorable for its quality, not its quantity.

He was an autocrat at heart, born in the wrong century and the wrong hemisphere. Or he was an earthy son of the Kansas sod, who found the most contentment when puttering about his Bluegrass farm, raising white-faced Herefords.

He was the sourest fellow ever to achieve fame and fortune. Or he was one of the funniest. Trainer Claude Vaughan once told of asking Rupp if he artificially inseminated his cattle. No, the coach replied, adding, "I like my

bulls to enjoy their work."

He was utterly rational and organized to the point of obsessiveness. Or he was superstitious, wearing that brown suit, stuffing buckeyes in his pockets, and looking for hairpins on game day, for good luck. (To improve his luck, acolytes took to strewing hairpins in his path.) The following may be attributed to superstition, or stinginess: "He lodged in the same old hotels across Dixie until they were condemned," Dinwiddie says.

He was a racist who resisted recruiting black players until his domain slid into decline. Or he was amenable to having black players — his teams played against blacks when other Southern teams wouldn't — and he was simply hamstrung by place and time. "That may be a cross around his neck," says Parsons. "People thought he was prejudiced, and he really was not."

Progressive as he was on the court, he was socially behind the times. Or he was simply ahead of his time: Nowadays, his politics sound more contemporary than his basketball. "Our sports program," he once declared, "is the last

Joe B. Hall joined Rupp's staff as an assistant in 1965.

vestige of free enterprise in America. Everything else has been fouled up in Washington, and too many people expect Washington to make a success of their lives."

He was a brilliant, perceptive student of human nature who missed nothing. (He once said you could judge a player's aggressiveness by the way he attacked his steak; he watched Hagan devour a steak and figure he'd do the same to opponents. Hagan, incidentally, ended up owning a chain of steak houses.) Or he was so blinded by his pursuit of victory that he missed the gamblers meddling with his players in the late 1940's, declaring, "The gamblers couldn't touch my boys with a 10-foot pole."

He was a towering egotist who loaded every pronouncement with Olympian import. Or he was simply an acerbic humorist whose audience didn't get it, owing to the pontifical trappings of the UK coaching job. (Pitino encountered this phenomenon when his every utterance, no matter how flip, was taken as Holy Writ by the more solemn fans.)

He was exactly what he seemed, a man incapable of artifice. Or he was an actor who grasped this: The only game bigger than basketball is life its own self.

Like the fictional detective John Shaft, it must be said that Adolph Rupp was a complicated man.

Or maybe not.

The thing he hated, above all, was losing. At anything.

Quoth Parsons: "He was energetic, and he loved to compete. ... He wanted to have the best tobacco crop on earth. He thought he had the best Hereford cows, and if he didn't he'd get rid of what he didn't like, genetically. ... In any facet of life, he wanted to compete and be the best. If it was making money, he wanted to make more than anyone else. If he was speaking before a crowd, he wanted more people there than Bobby Knight would have had there."

Rupp would abide none of sports' cheery bromides. "If it matters not who wins or loses," he asked, "what the hell is that scoreboard doing up there?"

"The eternal verity in Rupp's personality," Kindred wrote, "was his love of victory."

In that regard, his love was requited as much as any man's: 876 victories, four NCAA titles, a 129-game home-court winning streak.

Rupp's UK career, which stretched from 1930-72, was somewhat like his elocution: It rose in the middle. From 1946-54, his teams won 205 games and lost 20. He had three NCAA titlists, an NIT champion and an runner-up when, in the words of Beard, "the NIT was 20 times as large as the NCAA."

Rupp's impossible dream of perfection seemed at hand in 1954, when his team went 25-0. But the top stars, Hagan and Ramsey, were graduate students and ineligible for postseason play. UK decided to sit out the tournament; LaSalle, a 13-point loser to UK in the regular season, won the title. That indignity came on the heels of the 1953 season that wasn't (no team, owing to suspension, owing to booster payoffs to players). That indignity had come right after the exposure of the point-shaving scandals involving five UK players. So, Kentucky, for all its sheen, had to atone for its shame.

In Rupp's universe, atonement took one form: triumph. In 1958, he got it. His last champion was his least likely. The "Fiddlin' Five" of Adrian Smith, Vern Hatton, John Crigler, John Cox and Ed Beck upset Elgin Baylor and Seattle, 84-72, in the NCAA final in Louisville.

The next season, his team went to

The life and times of Adolph Rupp

1901: Born in Halstead, Kan., to Henry and Anna Rupp, as a first-generation American; he speaks only German before going to school; when Adolph is 9, his father dies, and the hard life on the farm gets harder.

1923: Graduates Phi Beta Kappa from the University of Kansas, where he studied economics and history — and basketball, under legendary coach Phog Allen.

1930: Receives master's degree in education from Columbia University; after three years of coaching high school in Freeport, Ill., he interviews at the University of Kentucky, declaring himself "the best damn coach in the nation;" he gets the job.

1931: Marries Esther Schmidt, a sweetheart from Freeport; they have one son, Herky.

1933: His third team is declared the national champions by the Helms Athletic Foundation.

1943: His team begins a record 129-game home-court winning streak that will last until 1955.

1946: Kentucky wins the NIT, a tournament more prestigious in those days than the NCAA.

1948, '49, '51, '58: His teams win NCAA championships.

1950: UK moves into 11,500-seat Memorial Coliseum.

1953: Wracked by disclosures of point-shaving, Kentucky is further wounded by news of booster payments to players, and is suspended for the season, in effect getting the "death penalty."

1954: Rupp's team is undefeated (25-0), but passes up postseason play because his top players are graduate students, and therefore ineligible; LaSalle, a 13-point loser to Kentucky in regular season, wins the NCAA's.

1955: Georgia Tech ends UK's 129-game home-court winning streak, 59-58.

1966: Rupp makes Final Four for last time, losing to Texas Western in a championship game famous as a black-white confrontation sometimes called "college basketball's Brown vs. the Board of Education."

1968: Inducted into the Basketball Hall of Fame.

1972: Forced into retirement, eventually becomes executive with two ABA teams, the Memphis Tams and Kentucky Colonels.

1976: Rupp attends the Kentucky-Kansas game as 23,500-seat Rupp Arena is dedicated.

1977: Dies of cancer and complications from diabetes on the night his old teams, Kentucky and Kansas, play each other, in his home state.

1997: Rupp's all-time victory record of 876 falls to another Phog Allen disciple, North Carolina's Dean Smith, who retires with 879 wins.

Vanderbilt 11-0, but played poorly in the first half. Parsons recalls Rupp turning to his assistant in the locker room and growling: "Harry, by God, I know what we ought to do. Let's just have these guys walk back out to the center of the floor and take their trousers off in front of all those people and just piss right there in the center of the floor, and then they can write home and say they did something."

Players were the natural targets of Rupp's sarcasm. So were referees. Parsons recalls a 1960 game in which Tulane's towering center, Jack Ardon, rather artlessly scored three straight baskets.

"That man's walking!" Rupp protested each time. Finally, he called timeout and sent Parsons to summon referee George Conley, a state senator from Ashland.

"Coach Rupp says, 'Sena-TOR,' and he lets that ring out. ..." says Parsons, who recalls the rest of the dialogue this way. ...

Rupp: "You know, you have proposed a $3 million road bill for those people up in Eastern Kentucky."

Conley (surprised): "Well, that's right."

Rupp: "I wanted you to know we don't need the damned thing."

Conley: "Well, why not?"

Rupp: "Well, by God, let 'em walk all over the state, like you're letting that big center walk every time he catches the ball."

"George gets tickled," Parsons says. "It wasn't funny to us. We never laughed at anything like that. ... George just went back out and laughed about it. The next time down, George calls walking on this big guy.

"That was his [Rupp's] method of being such a psychologist. ... He was always making his point just that way. He was more of an actor, I think, than anything else. I understood that more when I came back as an assistant coach. I realized that he was acting the entire time. He would have been a champion in Hollywood."

The old coach would never again be a national champion, though. He came closest in 1966 — with the team called Rupp's Runts — Pat Riley, Louie Dampier, Larry Conley, Tommy Kron and the tallest starter, 6-5 Thad Jaracz. (Such undersized teams weren't so strange in those days. Two years before,

In his final years at Kentucky, Rupp's legendary status had risen to that of a cultural icon.

UCLA won the title with a similar lineup.) For once, sentiment favored the 64-year-old coach and his overachievers.

In the championship game at College Park, Md., the all-white Kentucky team faced Texas Western, which used seven players, all black. Texas Western won, 72-65, in a game that still stands as one of basketball's watershed events.

Twenty years later, Dampier would say if the two teams had played 10 times, Kentucky would win nine. Riley, his roommate, thought Kentucky would lose 9 of 10, owing to Texas Western's mountainous motivation.

"Losing ... that year was the possibly biggest disappointment of my life," Rupp said, "because that was my best coaching job." (Rupp-watchers could find in that observation one of his least endearing traits: taking credit for the successes, blaming the players for the failures.)

People who know only one thing about Adolph Rupp know this: His all-white team lost to an all-black team, and he was cranky about it.

(Footnote in history: If Kentucky had not slipped past Duke, another all-white team, in the semifinals, Duke might have stood as the symbol of Southern sports segregation.)

"I don't think he ever recovered emotionally," Issel wrote in his biography.

The next season was Rupp's worst, 13-13, and intimations of mortality filled the air along Euclid Avenue, home of Memorial Coliseum.

Harry Lancaster, his old assistant, eventually ascended to the athletic director's post. In a book called *Adolph*

Rupp As I Knew Him, Lancaster would recall: "I think Adolph slipped a bit as a coach right after we had the Runts. We lost all those close games and he'd sit there on the bench late in the game and almost panic. He had lost his grip as a great coach. The players were aware of it. He would get his plays confused in practice sometimes...."

Rupp may have lost his courtside touch, but he was still practicing psychology rather effectively. When players sent Issel to complain about a strenuous running program enforced by assistant coach Joe Hall, Rupp persuaded Issel to run, not rebel. The payoff: Rupp would abet Issel's run for the UK career scoring record. (Issel got the record, 2,138 points.)

Issel's 1970 team was top-ranked, and Rupp's last shot at glory. But it fell, 106-100, to Jacksonville, one game short of the Final Four. The next year, UK lost to Western Kentucky 107-83 in the NCAA regionals. At one point, Rupp turned to his aides and said, "I don't know what to do."

That game was a close-to-home variation on the theme of Texas Western. All five Western starters were from Kentucky, and all were black. That fall, Rupp was as sore a loser as ever, grousing that some of Western's players weren't up to the academic standards at UK.

By then, Rupp was facing one of UK's unyielding standards: mandatory retirement at 70. His old mentor at Kansas, Phog Allen, had fought retirement fiercely: He was bodily removed from his office.

"If they retire me, they may as well take me on out to Lexington Cemetery," Rupp told Russell Rice, the UK sports publicist.

They did retire him, in March of 1972, in a graceless moment for all concerned. For consolation, Rupp sought other eminences. He threatened briefly to run for congress. "I've won 83 percent of everything I've ever been involved with," he said. But that idea quickly passed.

He kept an office at Memorial Coliseum, and he had a Sunday night TV show, declaiming on issues great and small. Regarding Pete Maravich's rumored $1 million pro deal, Rupp said, "If that's what he got, he's smarter than the fella that gave it to him."

He held administrative posts with two pro teams, the Memphis Tams and the Kentucky Colonels. He lived to see Rupp Arena open in 1976, though his

vision was failing and his health problems mounting.

A year later, he lay dying of cancer. Parsons and V.A. Jackson, the team doctor, went to see the old coach on his death bed. Jackson asked if there was anything he could do.

"He told Doc Jackson he wanted to get with all his buddies," Parsons says, "and he didn't want all this moaning and wailing if he didn't make it through this thing — he wasn't going to make it, and he knew it — he just wanted him to bring a little old flask of whiskey, and all his buddies just have a drink."

Whereupon Jackson asked the coach, "Do you want us to have a drink before or after the funeral?"

"Well, by God, I want you to have it before," Rupp replied. "I won't be with you afterwards."

On Saturday night, Dec. 10, 1977, Kentucky — a team 107 days away from the national championship — played at Kansas, his alma mater. UK won, 73-66. Upon landing at the airport back home, the word spread to the players. After four days in a coma, the old coach had died.

Somehow, even in a coma, he managed his last moment for maximum effect.

The Baron says good-bye to the Wildcat faithful in his final game at Memorial Coliseum in 1972.

Above: In the 1932-33 season, the Wildcats won 21 games and lost 3.

Below: The 1933-34 team posted a record of 16 wins and 1 loss.

Right: Paul McBrayer, an all-American guard in 1930.

(Left to right) Leroy Edwards, Garland Lewis and Courtland Bliss starred for the Wildcats in 1935.

Top: The 1945-46 Wildcats won 28 games, lost 2 and captured the NIT championship.

Bottom: Rupp's 1947-48 team won their first NCAA championship with 36 wins and 3 losses.

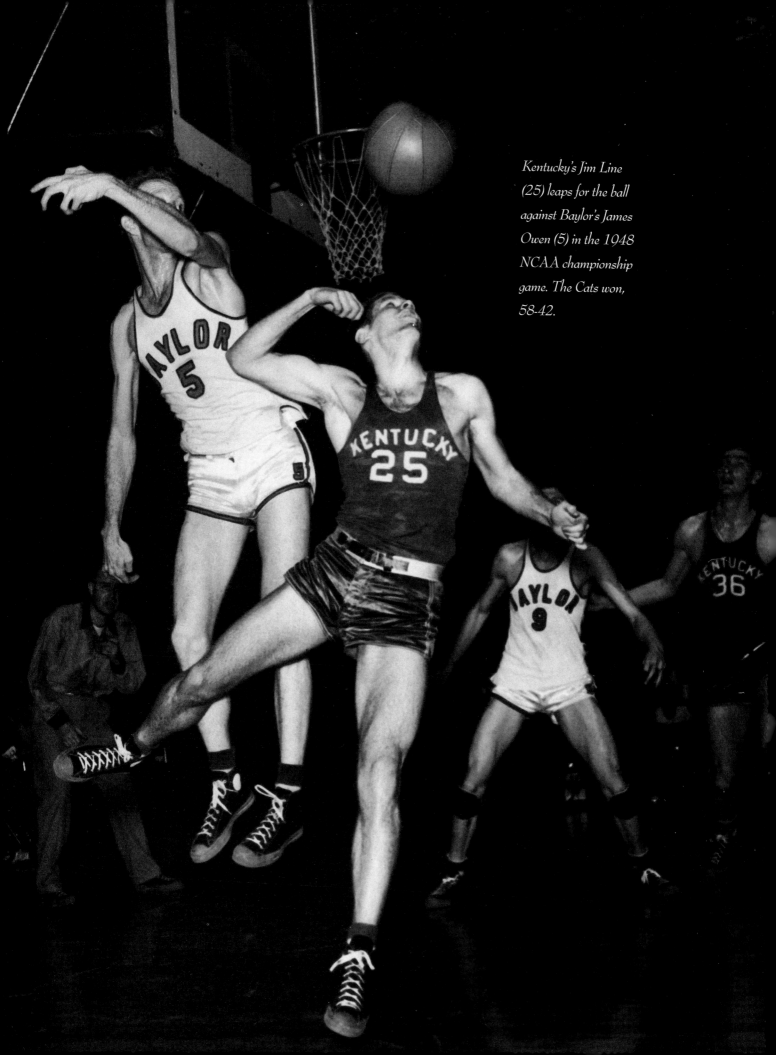

Kentucky's Jim Line (25) leaps for the ball against Baylor's James Owen (5) in the 1948 NCAA championship game. The Cats won, 58-42.

The Fabulous Five starred on the 1948 Olympics basketball team which Rupp coached.

Kentucky lost to the Phillips Oilers in the Finals of the 1948 Olympic Trials.

Right: Wah Wah Jones (27) and Alex Groza (15) look on as NYU's Ray Lumpp (24) grabs a rebound in the U.S. team's 59-57 win over Argentina in the 1948 Olympics.

The 1948-49 Wildcats won the NCAA championship again with a record of 32 wins and 2 losses.

Left: Ralph Beard, who had 23 points against the Phillips Oilers in the Olympic Trials, recovers after being floored by a pair of Oiler defenders.

Alex Groza (15) reaches for a rebound against Georgia in 1949.

Left: Jim Line (25) and Wah Wah Jones (27)
fight with Holy Cross' Bob Cousy for a loose
ball.

Rupp & Co. relish their second straight NCAA championship trophy after defeating Oklahoma A&M, 46-36.

Bill Spivey (11) launches a hook shot against CCNY in the 1950 NIT Tournament.

Top: The 1950-51 Wildcats won their third NCAA championship in four years with a record of 32 wins and 2 losses. Below: The 1951-52 Wildcats lost in the East Regionals of the NCAA Tournament, but finished with a record of 29 wins and 3 losses.

Bill Spivey (77) and Frank Ramsey (30) battle against Kansas State's Josh Gibson (21) for a rebound in Kentucky's 68-58 victory in the 1951 NCAA championship game.

The 1953-54 Wildcats' starting five: (left to right) Phil Grawemeyer, Bill Evans, Lou Tsioropoulos, Cliff Hagan and Frank Ramsey. Kentucky finished the season with a record of 25-0.

Left: Cliff Hagan scored 42 points against Tennessee in the 1952 SEC Tournament.

In the 1953-54 season, the Wildcats won their 16th SEC title in 21 seasons.

Right: Frank Ramsey, an all-American guard in 1952 and 1954.

The 1957-58 Wildcats won their fourth NCAA championship with a record of 23 wins and 6 losses.

Right: Ed Beck (34) battles for the rebound against Temple in the 1958 NCAA Final Four in Louisville.

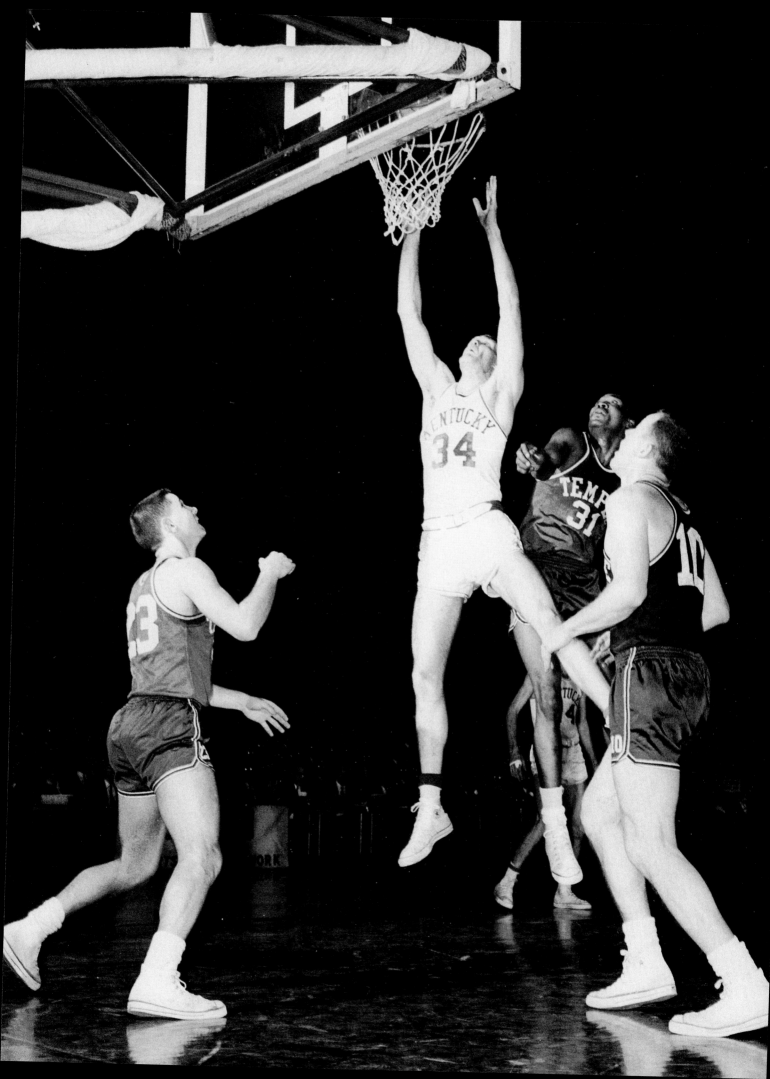

The 1961-62 Wildcats finished the season ranked No. 3 in the country with a record of 23 wins and 3 losses.

Left: Johnny Cox (24) reaches for a tip-in against Seattle in the 1958 NCAA championship game.

Rupp's Runts gather in the spotlight before the 1966 NCAA championship game against Texas Western.

The Wildcats' bench in the final minutes of the Texas Western game is shocked by their opponent's powerful showing. Texas Western eventually won, 72-65.

The 1965-66 Wildcats finished the season with a record of 27 wins and 2 losses.

*Right: Pat Riley (42) and Cliff Berger (45)
battle for a rebound against Texas Western in
the 1966 NCAA championship game.*

*Top: Rupp and assistant Joe B. Hall greet their 1969 freshmen recruits: (left to right) Steve Pen-
horwood, Larry Stamper, Dan Perry, Jim Andrews and Tom Payne. Below: Rupp's last team
— the 1971-72 Wildcats — finished the season ranked No. 3 with 23 wins and 3 losses.*

Heir
to the
Legacy

By Rick Bozich

Never be the man who follows The Man. In coaching, that is rule Number One. Let somebody else follow The Man. Then you follow that guy because chances are he'll be pushed to the sidelines quickly.

You can ask the man who followed John Wooden at UCLA. In fact, you can ask all seven of them. That is how many coaches who have tried to replace Wooden and the 10 NCAA championships that he won in Westwood.

Ask the folks in Green Bay about the daunting assignment of replacing Vince Lombardi. Phil Bengston is the guy who took the first shot. Dan Devine thought he'd make a run at it with the Packers until one day his dog ended up poisoned. Finally, nearly 30 years after Lombardi walked away with the first two Super Bowl trophies, Green Bay returned home with the 1997 Super Bowl trophy — which, of course, is named after Vince Lombardi.

Left: Joe B. Hall succeeded his mentor, Adolph Rupp, after the 1972 season.

In Alabama, the notion of following Bear Bryant has been more intimidating than taking the ball between the tackles on fourth-and- one.

Ray Perkins, a former Bryant player, volunteered to go first — and quickly returned to the pros. Bill Curry hung around for three years before leaving for Kentucky. Gene Stallings looked like he had it going when he won the 1992 national title, but he retired early to his farm in Texas.

Never be the man who follows The Man. Remember that advice.

And then remember to nod your head in admiration toward Joe B. Hall because he not only was a man who followed The Man, he was a man who did it well.

Imagine the circumstances when Hall took over the University of Kentucky program in 1972. He would replace Adolph Rupp, who won 876 games, which at the time was more games than any coach who ever worked with a whistle and clipboard. Four of those games that Rupp won came in the NCAA championship game. Only Wooden won more titles.

Joe B. Hall would replace a coach whose name was revered for basketball greatness from Ashland to Hopkinsville as well as from Boston to Los Angeles. You think of Kentucky basketball and you think of Rupp's players flashing down the court as the coach in the trademark brown suit sat on the sidelines admiring the dynasty he had created.

Joe B. Hall would replace the coach who had brought Beard and Groza and Hagan and Ramsey and Hatton and Nash and Riley and Dampier and Issel and so many other wonderful players to Lexington.

And get this: Joe B. Hall would do this in an atmosphere where the world knew that Rupp did not want to be watching from the sidelines as a retired coach. The world knew this because Rupp admitted his displeasure to anybody that asked. The world knew this if it watched any television because even

Joe B. Hall played briefly for Rupp and later returned as an assistant for 7 seasons.

during his first season of enforced retirement Rupp continued to appear on television show that was just as popular as Hall's TV show.

So Joe B. Hall not only followed The Man. He followed The Man who watched every move he made.

This was a task as formidable as the task of following Wooden, Lombardi or Bryant. But, looking back at the 13-season Joe B. Hall Era of UK basketball, we know that this was an impossible mission that Hall made possible.

We know this if we look at the Joe B. Hall Era in traditional terms. The validation of any coach comes with an NCAA championship. Hall won his in

1978, when his powerful Wildcats' team defeated Duke, 94-88, in St. Louis. Not only was this Kentucky's first NCAA championship in 20 years, it was the school's first in the modern era of integrated rosters and schools taking the game seriously on nearly every camp. No longer were the basketball teams in the Southeastern Conference coached by guys farmed out from the football team. Joe B. Hall competed against the Charles Barkleys, Dominique Wilkins and C.M. Newtons of the basketball world.

If numbers are what you need to be convinced of a coach's success, Hall has an equipment bag full that he can show you. In addition to the 1978 champions, he took teams to the NCAA Final Four in 1975 and 1984. In 13 seasons, he won 297 games, a victory percentage of nearly 75 percent. Four times he was named Southeastern Conference Coach of the year. His teams won part of eight SEC titles. It is not a problem uncovering numbers that prove how well Hall did a difficult job.

But many coaches have numbers, championships, conference titles and coaching awards. Hall should be remembered for more than beating Duke or handling Auburn in the SEC championship game.

Tubby Smith will become Kentucky's first African-American men's basketball coach this season. Hardly anybody questioned the decision of athletics director C.M. Newton to hire Smith to replace Rick Pitino last spring. Any student of UK basketball should pause to give Joe B. Hall credit for beginning the successful integration of the Kentucky program.

It was Rupp who brought the first black basketball player — Tom Payne — to Lexington. But after that moved failed to work out, Hall is the coach who welcomed players such as Merion Haskins, Larry Johnson, Jack Givens, James Lee, Dwane Casey, Truman Claytor, Sam Bowie and so many others into the program, and then helped them succeed. He brought Leonard Hamilton onto his staff as the program's first black assistant coach.

These are significant changes sometimes forgotten today, but for Hall in 1972 this was something he knew was right. Even Cawood Ledford, long the popular radio voice of the Wildcats, has written that Hall is the man who successfully integrated the UK basketball program. History should note that.

Spend time with any college basketball program today and you will quickly discover the season never ends. Shooting and dribbling are only a part of the preparation for a long season. Weights must be lifted. Rope should be jumped. Running is essential. Conditioning is critical to the success of any team.

Joe B. Hall is the coach who brought a sophisticated training system to the Kentucky basketball program. When other coaches rolled their eyes at all of the extra lifting and running that Hall demanded and wondered if the coach was transforming his players into brutes, the coach simply winked. He wanted to be certain that he had a fresh team in March. And, usually, he did.

In the beginning, skeptics wondered if Hall was determined to burn his team out. Today every nationally recognized team trains as relentlessly as Hall started training his Kentucky teams in the early 1970's. Hall was at the forefront of this trend.

And any student of sports knows that Joe B. Hall should be admired for another thing: For the way he showed how to live with expectations of great-

Hall and his team celebrate after winning the UKIT Tournament in 1977.

ness while following a legend.

No doubt sometimes this made the coach cranky. People who knew him well say he wasn't nearly as outgoing as the head coach as he was when he was Rupp's top assistant. The crankiness in Hall also showed when he continued to resist initiating a regular-season series with Louisville, a series which became an immense success the second it was created in 1983.

But there were often reasons for Hall to be cranky. When he took over at Kentucky coach in 1972 Adolph Rupp himself was available to comment about decisions Joe Hall made. In time Hall joked about this.

In 1975, Hall took his team to the NCAA Final Four. The Wildcats played UCLA in the championship game in San Diego. A day before the tipoff, Wooden announced the game would be his last as the UCLA coach. Hall joked that there was only one man qualified to follow John Wooden. That man was Joe B. Hall, the basketball coach with experience following a legend.

Kyle Macy, a sophomore on the 1978 national championship team, was Hall's leader on the court.

Hall tolerated the occasional conflicts because coaching and playing basketball in Kentucky is what he dreamed of as a boy. He grew up like so many Kentucky boys, with his ear squeezed against the radio listening to Adolph Rupp's teams on the radio. For Hall, the small town was Cynthiana, tobacco country, about 30 miles north of Lexington in Harrison County. Hall's father was Charles Hall, twice the county sheriff as well as the owner of a dry-cleaning plant.

In Cynthiana, Joe B. Hall was an example of what any coach would order from any student athlete. Three years he lettered in basketball. Three years he lettered in football. Hall was just warming up. He also captained both teams. He was voted president of the senior class. And he wanted to play for the Kentucky Wildcats.

Adolph Rupp gave him a chance. But when Hall got to UK in the late 1940's the squad was packed with talent as well as with veterans of World War II. Perhaps you have heard of a few of them   Ralph Beard, Alex Groza, Wah Wah Jones, Cliff Barker, Kenny Rollins and Dale Barnstable.

The basketball world called them "the Fabulous Five." Hall called himself "the eighth of the five." You can see him, wearing jersey No. 31, sitting in the front row, between Beard and Garland Townes, in the front row of the team picture when Kentucky won its second consecutive NCAA title by defeating Oklahoma A&M in 1949.

How badly did Joe B. Hall want to play for the Wildcats?

You be the judge. As a freshman Hall underwent a tonsillectomy on a Friday. By Wednesday he was back at practice. By the end of the same week he returned to the hospital because of the bleeding. That was not Hall's only trip to the hospital that season. Doctors also treated him for a sprained right ankle and infected left foot.

But no amount of treatment or extraordinary conditioning could get Joe B. Hall into that formidable Kentucky lineup. As much as Hall loved Kentucky, Hall also loved competing and playing. He left UK for the Uni-

Hall listens while Bobby Knight chews out a referee in 1984.

versity of the South in Sewanee, Tenn., where he is still recognized as one of the school's all-time best players.

Before Hall started coaching he had to discover how much he loved the game. You discover your love by trying something other than basketball. Joe B. Hall sold ketchup and other items for five years. It taught him how much he loved basketball. And it taught him how to sell many things — including himself.

From there, Hall's life became strictly dribbling. He coached his first team in high school in Shepherdsville, Ky., in 1956. This was a coach in a hurry. After two seasons he departed for Regis College in Denver, which hired Hall as an assistant coach. Within one year he was the head man. Five solid seasons at Regis gave Hall the credentials to get the head job at Central Missouri State, where he followed Gene Bartow.

Finally, in 1965, Joe B. Hall returned to Kentucky. He returned to work with Adolph Rupp, who asked him to become one of his assistant coaches. It is no coincidence that Joe B. Hall's first season as one of Rupp's assistant was one of the most glorious seasons Rupp ever enjoyed.

During the 1964-65 season, the

year before Hall arrived, Kentucky lost 10 of 25 games. The Wildcats, who started Louie Dampier, Pat Riley, Tommy Kron, Larry Conley and John Adams, lost in the final of the UK Invitation Tournament. They were beaten by 19 points at Tennessee and by 16 points in Florida. Three straight times they lost in mid-February. They were not invited to the NCAA Tournament.

Enter Joe B. Hall. One of the first things he talked to Rupp about was the importance of a rigorous pre-season conditioning program. Let the rest of the basketball world wait to train when practice began. Let's get everybody in shape earlier in the fall so October and November can be used for teaching basketball.

Eventually Rupp agreed to the wisdom his aggressive young assistant was preaching. In 1965-66, Kentucky replaced one man (Adams with Thad Jaracz) from the lineup of the previous disappointing season. Kentucky started the season with nobody in its lineup taller than 6 feet 5 inches. Kentucky also started its season with 10 consecutive double-figure victories. Many teams were taller than Kentucky. Few teams were in better condition. The

Hall visits with Louisville coach Denny Crum before their game in the 1984 Mideast Regionals Final.

Wildcats were ranked Number One throughout most of the winter, refusing to lose until Tennessee defeated them in the next to last game of the regular season. Their season ended with a runner-up finish in the NCAA Tournament.

Rupp would coach six more seasons, ignoring any hints of retirement until he was 70. Hall was only an assistant coach, but he was a man with head coaching ambition. In April of 1969, he left UK for about a week to become the head coach at St. Louis University. Only after administrators at UK, including Rupp, convinced Hall that he would become the next head coach did Hall agree to return.

Hall was a man who understood how rapidly the game and American society was changing. When Kentucky lost that 1966 NCAA championship game to a Texas Western squad with five black starting player, Hall recognized the shift in the college basketball landscape. He also saw the increased interest other schools in the Southeastern Conference were taking in basketball.

No longer could Kentucky pick and choose every basketball recruit it wanted. The Wildcats' approach to recruiting would have to be upgraded and expanded to search more states and more summer camps. Hall is the guy who brought increased organization to UK's recruiting efforts. He went into Illinois to find Dan Issel. In one of his early years as an assistant coach Hall bragged that he traveled 25,000 miles to watch 175 games and scout 2,500 players. The army of recruiters who travel the country at that pace today can credit Hall for this push toward wall-to-wall recruiting.

Hall's hard work delivered dividends. In 1971, many argued that Kentucky signed the best recruiting class in

America. With help from Hall, Kentucky landed the Mr. Basketball in four states — Kentucky [Jimmy Dan Connors], Indiana [Mike Flynn], Ohio [Kevin Grevey] and Illinois [Bob Guyette]. By now, many people had noticed what Hall had done and believed he was the man to replace The Man.

One person who was not wondering about that was Adolph Rupp. His 876 victories, 27 SEC titles, 4 NCAA championships, 1 NIT title and 23 all-Americans were not enough.

Rupp was prepared to coach forever. Only mandatory retirement convinced Rupp to step down after the 1972 season.

To replace Rupp, Kentucky turned to the former ketchup salesman who grew up listening to the Wildcats from his bedroom in Cynthiana, Ky.

The job of replacing a legend was tough enough, but sometimes Rupp made it tougher than it needed to be. He did that by making sure the world understood he wasn't really ready to step aside. Kentucky lost three of its first four games under Hall and many people talked about how much the great man was missed. After Hall rallied his team for a strong finish, a share of the

SEC championship and a runner-up finish in the NCAA Mideast Regional, somebody asked Rupp what he thought of Kentucky's 20-8 performance in Hall's debut. "A disappointing season," is what Rupp called it.

Hall's second season was just as difficult. Kentucky split 26 games. Twice the Wildcats lost to Alabama. After losing four in a row at the end of February, they had to defeat Mississippi State in the final game of the season to avoid a losing record. Rupp offered not a word of praise or criticism of Hall's performance. A few people interpreted his silence as criticism. Joe B. Hall learned quickly about the difficulty of being the man who followed The Man.

But then Joe B. Hall did something many coaches who follow famous men have failed to do — he started winning. He started winning his way, with his players. In 1975, Hall took a team of courageous veterans and frisky freshman and drove them all the way to the NCAA Final Four.

He stood at center court at Assembly Hall in Bloomington and told Indiana coach Bob Knight that he would not back down even as the Hoosiers were pounding Kentucky by 24 points. This was an important moment for Hall because three months later, in Dayton in the championship game of the NCAA Mideast Regional, Kentucky upset an unbeaten and top-ranked Indiana team for the right to advance to the NCAA Final Four. This was no longer Adolph Rupp's basketball program. This program belonged to Joe B. Hall. Now there was no doubt.

In that memorable third season, Kentucky beat Syracuse in the semifinals before falling to UCLA and Wooden, 92-85, in a brilliant championship game.

But while finishing second, Hall created something that would eventually help him finish first — in Rick Robey, Jack Givens, Mike Phillips and James Lee, he put together a talented group of freshmen who were savvy seniors when UK began the 1977-78 season ranked the Number One-ranked team in the land.

College basketball writers expected Kentucky to win the national title. Opposing coaches liked the Wildcats, too. Expectations raged within UK fans.

Sam Bowie receives final instructions from Hall during a second-half timeout against Florida State in 1980.

In a situation where greatness was expected, greatness is what Hall demanded. Sometimes winning when you are expected to win can be the most difficult coaching assignment in sports. But Hall had constructed this team carefully. If Hall did not embrace the expectations, neither did he run from them.

Kyle Macy, the son of a coach, arrived as a transfer from Purdue to serve as a leader along with the four seniors. Truman Claytor provided poise and persistence at the other guard spot. Jay Shidler made difficult shots, while Fred Cowan and LaVon Williams collected difficult rebounds. At times all 14 members of the team contributed.

Kentucky began that championship quest by handling Southern Methodist, Indiana and Kansas. Fourteen consecutive opponents fell before the Wildcats were upset by Alabama. Observers wondered if Hall was driving this team too relentlessly, but Hall knew there are no celebrations in March for teams that do not show determination in January and February.

On Feb. 11 Kentucky lost another basketball game at Louisiana State. The Wildcats lost, 95-94, even though all five LSU starters fouled out of the game. Hall took a long look at his team and wondered if they were destined to become the Foldin' Five. There would be no acceptance of defeat. The best way Hall knew how to coach a team was to drive them, so drive this group he did.

Kentucky finished the regular season with eight more victories. They were the team to beat in the NCAA Tournament. And they were nearly the first team beaten. Florida State led UK, 39-32, at halftime of a first-round NCAA game played in Knoxville.

That is the day Joe B. Hall showed he was not afraid of taking a chance. That is the day Joe B. Hall won the 1978 NCAA title. To start the second half he benched Robey, Givens and Claytor, replacing them with Dwane Casey, Cowan and Williams in a lineup that also included Macy and Phillips.

Twenty minutes from a jarring elimination and the largest disappointment of Joe Hall's coaching career, UK rallied for a nine-point victory. Success over Miami of Ohio and then Michigan State, led by freshman point guard

Kentucky's 92-90 win over Indiana in the 1975 Mideast Regionals halted the Hoosiers' 34-game winning streak.

Dirk Minnifield (10) was a playmaker for the Wildcats. UK had to score 8 points in the closing minutes to ensure the win against Indiana in 1975.

Truman Claytor (22) drives against Duke in the 1978 NCAA championship game.

Earvin Johnson came next.

At the Final Four in St. Louis, the Wildcats were matched first against Arkansas. Observers wondered if a Kentucky team known for its strength and power — created by Hall's demand for conditioning — would struggle against an Arkansas team that Eddie Sutton had built to feature quickness and guard play. No problem. Kentucky could play the same, slow or fast. Champions always can. The Wildcats beat Arkansas, 64-59.

The NCAA championship game would be another motivational challenge for the coach. Kentucky was supposed to win — and win big against a Duke team dominated by underclassmen. Media covering the Final Four portrayed Duke as the team having all the fun while a crabby group of Kentucky players labored under smothering expectations.

If the expectations smothered Kentucky, the video tapes show little evidence of it. Jack Givens came out firing and never stopped. He made 18 of 27 shots, scoring 41 points as Kentucky won, 94-88, for the school's fifth national championship — and Hall's first. The Wildcats celebrated as enthusiastically as any national champion ever had.

Forgotten in the talk of Kenucky's season of celebration and non-stop expectations was what Hall achieved. Unlike what we have seen at UCLA, Green Bay and Alabama, Hall had proven that it was possible to successfully be the man who followed The Man.

Hall stayed at Kentucky for seven more seasons, winning at least a part of four more SEC titles. He made another trip to the Final Four, but Kentucky missed 30 of 33 shots in a remarkable second half and lost to Georgetown, the eventual 1984 NCAA champion, 53-40.

Hall coached one more season, a season in which little was expected from the Wildcats because they were replacing three starters. And Kentucky was fortunate to sneak into the 1985 NCAA Tournament with a 16-12 record

But once Hall's team was rewarded with that NCAA bid, they played as if they believed they were a Number One seed, defeating Washington and Nevada Las Vegas, while making an unexpected visit to the Sweet Sixteen. The 1985 Final Four was played in Lexington. Maybe the Wildcats could wiggle into a trip to their homecourt.

Not this time. Hall's final UK team, the one that started Kenny Walker, Winston Bennett, Todd Bearup, Roger Harden and Ed Davender, was beaten by St. John's in the first round of the West Regional. After the game, Joe B.

Mike Flynn drives for a basket against UCLA in the 1975 NCAA championship game, which the Bruins won, 92-85. Flynn finished with 10 points.

(Left to right) Rick Robey, James Lee and Jack (Goose) Givens savor their win against Duke in the 1978 NCAA championship game. The Wildcats won, 94-88.

Hall surprised the basketball world by announcing that he had resigned.

Long before Hall's retirement announcement, he often enjoyed playing with reporters who pressed him to reveal what the "B" in his name represented. Instead of confessing that it was short for "Beaman," Hall tried to argue that it was short for "Bashful."

Kevin Grevey (35) watches as Bob Guyette (45) drives for a basket. Guyette scored 16 points against UCLA in 1975.

When pressed further for the truth, Hall said, "Basketball. Joe Basketball Hall."

You could remember him that way, Joe Basketball Hall.

Or you could remember him as the man who showed the world it was possible to follow The Man. Either way, he was the coach who followed up the four NCAA championships won by Adolph Rupp by winning another, thereby setting the stage for the glory pursued by Rick Pitino.

Jack Givens shoots from the corner against Duke in the 1978 NCAA championship game. Givens scored 41 points against the Blue Devils.

*Kyle Macy's confidence and playmaking
skills were keys to the Wildcats' title in 1978.*

Rick Robey, who scored 3 dunks against Nevada-Las Vegas in 1978, joined Mike Phillips in Kentucky's original "Twin Towers."

Kyle Macy soars for a layup against Arkansas in the 1978 NCAA Final Four.

Kyle Macy sinks one of his 10 "clutch" free throws against Michigan State in the 1978 Mideast Regional Final.

Seven-foot-1 Sam Bowie, an all-American center in 1981, scored 19 points against Ohio State in 1980.

*Sam Bowie makes this basket against LSU's
Ethan Martin (21) and Greg Cook (43) in
1981 look easy.*

Sam Bowie pulls down a rebound against Georgia in 1984.

Left: Jim Master, who saw many Notre Dame
games as a youngster in Fort Wayne, Ind., hit
on 4 of six shots against the Irish in 1982.

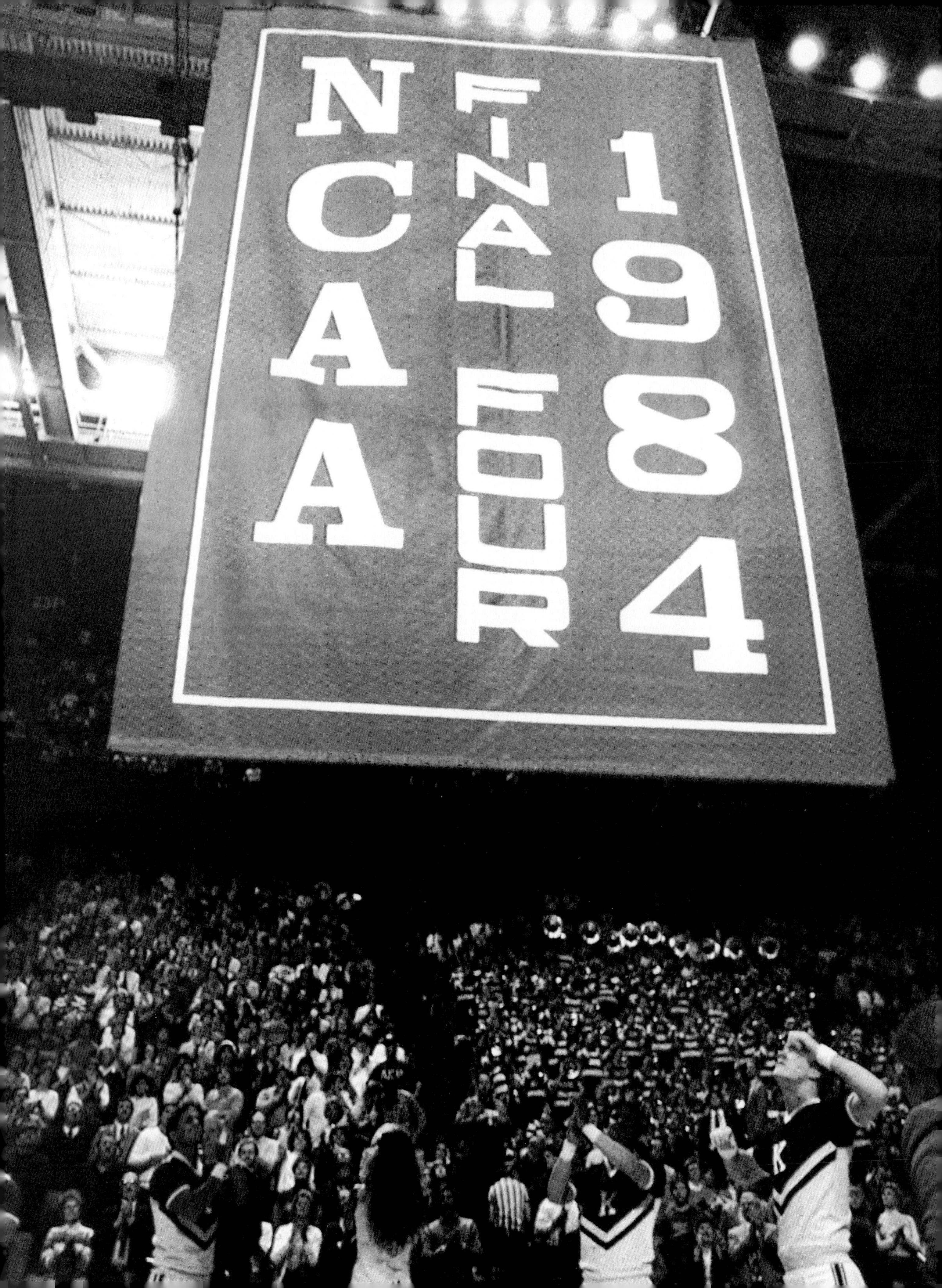
NCAA
FINAL FOUR
1984

Melvin Turpin keeps Georgetown's Patrick Ewing in check during their 1984 Final Four meeting. Ewing only scored 8 points in that game.

Left: The Wildcats lost to Georgetown, 53-40, in the 1984 Final Four.

Sam Bowie (31) and Melvin Turpin (54) formed Kentucky's "Twin Towers II."

Left: Melvin Turpin, who awaits a team-
mate's pass, scored over 15 points a game in
1984.

The Twin Towers, Sam Bowie and Melvin Turpin, during a preseason jog in 1983.

*Left: Kenny Walker scored 32 points and
pulled down 15 rebounds in an 81-68 loss to
Louisville in 1984.*

Joe B. Hall enjoys the crowning moment of his career following the Wildcats' win over Duke in the 1978 NCAA championship game in St. Louis.

After his retirement in 1985, Joe B. Hall's banner was added to the rafter's in Rupp Arena.

The Bluegrass Savior

By Mark Woods

He wore a blue shirt with a white collar and, of course, a conservative, classically cut, dark suit.

In the early years, Rick Pitino had been an Armani man. By the end, though, he had graduated to $3,000 Brionis. Straight from Italy. Just like Pierce Brosnan's 007.

"You're never going to take the New York out of me," he had said once. "I'm very pro-Italian. I like Gucci shoes and Armani ties."

Eight years in Lexington didn't change that. Pitino still had a lot of New York in him. A reminder of that came every time he opened his mouth and talked about playing "Indianer" or "Utar" or being sent out west in the NCAA "Toynmanent."

But those eight years did change a lot of other things, including the face of Kentucky basketball. It wasn't just that Pitino took a once-proud program, lifted it out of probation and back atop the basketball world. It wasn't just the five Southeastern Conference Tournament titles, the three Final Fours, the two national championship games or even the 1996 title.

Pitino gave UK a complete makeover. He sandblasted away that stodgy, uptight, no-fun-allowed image and replaced it with three-point shots, full-court pressure, denim uniforms, Alan Parsons "Eye in the Sky" introductions, celebrities on the bench and seemingly a controversy-a-day.

They were eight wild, wonderful years. And they also changed the face of Pitino. They put a couple wrinkles on that boyish mug. They turned him into a 44-year-old coach who had not only stuck around long enough to shed some of those early labels — "Larry Brown on training wheels" — but actually had considered settling into Lexington for the rest of his career.

He had turned down $30 million

from the New Jersey Nets one year earlier, saying he went with his heart and decided to stay in Kentucky.

But on May 6, 1997, he decided it was time to move on. That morning, before making the announcement that he was going to become the next coach of the Boston Celtics, he got ready for his last day of work as UK basketball coach.

It was no coincidence that he wore a blue-and-white shirt. There is no such thing as coincidence in Pitino's life. Everything is planned. Even attire. Especially attire. The walk-in closet at his Lexington home had more than a hundred shirts, all of them hung facing in the same direction and all arranged by color and designer.

He chose to wear blue and white. It went nicely with the ring.

For a while, it looked as if the fact that his right ring finger was bare might be his legacy: The Best Coach Who Never Won a Title. It had become a running joke, one that Pitino even told on himself to take some of the sting away.

"When I met the pope, I leaned over and kissed his ring," he said after returning from a preseason trip to Italy in the summer of 1995. "Then he looked at my hand to do the same, and

he said, 'Oh, you don't have a ring.' "

He, of course, got his ring that next spring. And on May 6, 1997, there it was, glinting in a flurry of strobes as he sat down at a table on the east concourse of Memorial Coliseum. Outside the building sat dozens of satellite trucks. Inside, 22 TV cameras were lined up. Around the state, thousands of fans were bracing themselves. One had even called UK athletic director C.M. Newton that day and suggested devising a state tax to match the Boston Celtics' offer.

"Thank you all for coming," Pitino began, his voice unusually tense. "Eight years ago ..."

"Sir," interrupted an operator's voice contraption on the table set up to beam Pitino's words to reporters around the country. "Are you ready to begin?"

When Pitino continued, it quickly became clear that this was it. He was ready to *end*.

"Eight years ago, C.M. and I talked about the Kentucky situation," he said. "I remember it like it was yesterday, because it has gone by so fast. ..."

There will never be another era in Kentucky basketball like it. Or at least Big Blue

Kentucky athletic director C.M. Newton presents Rick Pitino with a UK lapel pin, welcoming him as the school's new basketball coach in 1989.

fans had better hope there isn't.

You see, part of the magic of the Pitino Era isn't how high he lifted the program, it is how low it began.

The *Sports Illustrated* cover said it all. "KENTUCKY'S SHAME."

It was the spring of 1989. Kentucky basketball was known for sending a package containing $1,000 to the father of Chris Mills, for helping Eric Manuel on a college entrance exam and, perhaps most stunning of all, for losing.

The team had just gone 13-19,

UK's first losing season since 1926-27. Eddie Sutton had been forced out as coach.

The program had hit rock bottom. And the NCAA was piling on sanctions that seemed to make certain it would stay there: three years' probation, a two-year ban from the NCAA Tournament, one year without live TV.

Anyone want this job?

Lute Olson didn't. P.J. Carlesimo didn't.

For that matter, the new athletic director at UK kind of wondered why

Pitino did.

Newton didn't try to ignore the program's problems and paint a glowing picture when he flew to New York to meet with the coach of the New York Knicks.

To the contrary, he explained how

Pitino's first team, in 1989-90, had more coaches and staff members than players.

the scandal and impending probation had scared away most of the good players, how Mills and Manuel had transferred after being ruled ineligible, how

whoever accepted this job would have to play Louisville, Indiana, Kansas and North Carolina during his first season.

"You're not going to win but three or four games," Newton said. "We have major problems."

The way legend has it, after a moment of awkward silence, Newton looked at Pitino and said: "And we can't figure out why the head coach of the New York Knicks, on the threshold of winning a championship, would ever want to come into this mess."

There were many reasons, but the

biggest was the challenge of taking what Pitino called "the Roman Empire of college basketball" and rebuilding it to its former glory.

The fact that Kentucky was down didn't scare Pitino away. It drew him to the Bluegrass.

It was what made Pitino, then 36 years old, decide to leave the city he was born in and the job he had dreamed of, to travel 700 miles into the heart of America.

On June 1, 1989, he agreed to come to a place where people still expected national titles, even though there hadn't been one there since 1978. A place that would soon be on probation. A place that had been making news for all the wrong reasons.

"I promise to you people in this room today, you'll see Kentucky on the cover of *Sports Illustrated* once again," he said the next day. "And it will be cutting down certain nets."

He had a plan. He wanted to get Kentucky off probation. He wanted to get good players. He wanted to have fun.

He went about it in reverse order. Fun first. The rest later.

That first team will forever hold a place in the heart of UK fans and Piti-

no. He mentioned it the day he resigned, saying that he had woke that morning and taken a look at a picture in his bedroom a team photo of the 1989-90 Wildcats.

"I saw more people in suits than uniforms," he said with a smile. "God, we have so many great memories here at Kentucky. I don't know where to begin."

How about at the start?

Nov. 28, 1989. Ohio University was in town for the first game of the Pitino era. All the fans at Rupp Arena were wearing Pitino masks, courtesy of a local grocery in town. The public address announcer bellowed an NBA-like introduction: "The Rick Pitino era at the University of Kentucky is about to begin! Let's give a great welcome to Riiiiiick Pitinoooooooo!"

Pitino had some adjusting to do. At one point, he tried calling for a 20-second timeout, forgetting that there was no such thing in college basketball. Still, that night gave a sign of things to come. It was filled with hustle, frenetic defense and three-point shots.

And it ended with Kentucky winning, 76-63.

It would turn out to be the first of 219 victories for Pitino at Kentucky.

It's hard to say which was the best of

Pitino's on-the-court intensity, off-the-court fun-loving ways — and winning — made him a folk hero among Wildcats fans.

the 219.

The biggest? That's easy. That would be the one played April 1, 1996, in a gym across the river from where Pitino grew up.

It wasn't a picturesque game. Syracuse committed 24 turnovers. Kentucky made only 28 of 73 shots. Still, the Wildcats had defense, which, as Pitino would point out later in one of many NBA references, was what the Chicago Bulls used to win their championships.

Pretty or ugly. Offense or defense. Who cares? The bottom line was a 76-67 victory. Pitino had become the promise keeper. He had capped off a

season that included 27 consecutive victories and the first sweep of the SEC regular season in 40 years by delivering to Big Blue Fans their first national title in 18 years.

That was the biggest victory. But it was hardly the best.

Maybe it was that first-year meeting with LSU. The Tigers rolled into town on Feb. 15, 1990 with a trio of future NBA players. Shaquille O'Neal and Stanley Roberts in the frontcourt. Chris Jackson in the backcourt.

Kentucky countered with a roster whose tallest player, Reggie Hanson, stood 6-foot-7.

Yet, somehow the group nicknamed "The Bombinos" managed to win, 100-95. They would go on to finish that year 14-14. The sweetest .500 season UK had ever seen.

Maybe it was "The Mardi Gras Miracle." It was four years to the day after the upset of LSU at Rupp Arena. Kentucky was at Baton Rouge, down by 31 points, 15:42 remaining.

Then it happened. The Wildcats, clad in new shorts with wild blue and

Bill Keightley, who has served as the Wildcats' equipment manager since 1972, is often referred to as "Mr. Wildcat."

white stripes, came back with a flurry of — you guessed it — defense and three-pointers. With 19 seconds remaining, Walter McCarty made a shot from the corner that gave UK a 96-95 lead. And when the final buzzer sounded, they had won, 99-95 — the biggest road comeback in Division I basketball history.

Or how about those Louisville games?

There was a time when UK was afraid of playing its intrastate rival. It had to be dragged back into a yearly meeting kicking and screaming in 1983. U of L and Denny Crum had the state's hip program. UK was considered tired and stale. Pitino changed that in a hurry.

He lost the first meeting. But on Dec. 29, 1990, he took his team to Freedom Hall and knocked off an undefeated Louisville team, 93-85. At that moment, the tone of the series changed.

Pitino would win six of the of the last seven meetings with U of L, five of the last six against Arkansas and Indiana and the last nine against Tennessee.

That's not to say that all the victories were easy. How about that 1995 SEC Tournament title game? Down by 19 in the first half to Arkansas, UK made it to overtime, only to fall behind by nine again before winning, 95-93, sending Pitino sprinting onto the court, arms spread wide, to give Anthony Epps a big hug for his critical steal.

Or what about the losses? There were only 50 of them in eight years. But they often were spectacular. And in their own way, they usually were more revealing than any victory.

Take what happened in Pitino's fifth game as UK coach. He took the players he had inherited — "short, slow people who didn't really know how to play that system," is how he would later describe them — and headed to Kansas to play a team that was on top of the college basketball world.

He had Richie Farmer, John Pelphrey, Deron Feldhaus and Sean Woods and the rest of "The Bombinos" come out pressing. He had them continue to press even when it resulted in them falling behind by 20, 30 and 40 points. And when Jayhawks coach Roy Williams suggested that Pitino might

Pitino's courtside theatrics provided many great photo opportunities for newspapers and magazine photographers.

want to back off and maybe coast to a more respectable finish, Pitino responded with something not fit for print.

Kansas won, 150-95. It was the worst defeat in UK history. Yet, it told you a lot about Pitino. He had a plan. And he was going to stick to it no matter what.

It was 364 days later when UK and Kansas met again. This time the Wildcats won, 88-71.

Of course, there was The Loss. The one people will be talking about for decades. It was the next year, Pitino's third on the job. The Wildcats came off

Joanne and Rick Pitino visited the Pope in the Summer of 1995. A popular story among Kentucky fans is that after the Pitinos kissed the Pope's ring, the Pope looked at Pitino's hand to do the same, then said, "Oh, you don't have a ring." But less than 10 months later, Pitino finally got his ring.

probation and roared to within one game of the Final Four.

March 28, 1992. The East Regional in Philadelphia. Kentucky vs. Duke.

That, of course, was the game Christian Laettner took a length-of-the-court inbounds pass from Grant Hill, spun around at the top of the key, fired up a jump shot over two UK defenders.

If the home run that Bobby Thomson hit to send the Giants to the 1951 World Series was "The Shot Heard 'Round the World," then the 17-footer that propelled Duke into the 1992 Final Four was "The Shot *Seen* 'Round the World."

It is being replayed, dissected, discussed to this day. It gave Duke a 104-103 victory, ending what some call the greatest college basketball game ever.

Kentucky returned home, retired the jerseys of its four seniors the members

Pitino's post-game radio shows with longtime Wildcats announcer Cawood Ledford were a popular event for Kentucky fans.

of the original Pitino team — and buried the past.

"This is the last time I'll mention the NCAA probation," Pitino said. "It is over and will not happen again. Kentucky's shame is gone."

The Wildcats would make it to the Final Four the next year. In fact, they would go three of the final four Pitino years. And by his final season, Georgia Tech's Bobby Cremins would say: "Rick is the man right now. At one time John Wooden was the man, and Dean Smith and Bobby Knight and Mike Krzyzewski. Well, right now Rick is the man. He's changed college basketball."

Cremins was talking about the style of play Pitino developed. The pressing. The speed. The no-fear shooting.

And while all of that certainly was part of Pitino's stay at Kentucky, it was so much more than that.

It was an eight-year Broadway show. With Pitino playing the leading man.

It was the way the commonwealth fell for a Yankee. And vice versa.

After a trip to the Final Four in 1993, the Kentucky student body began to fall in love with their coach.

It was Pitino riding a motorcycle onto the court for Midnight Madness.

It was Pitino leaving the Armanis at home for the final UK game against Alabama coach Wimp Sanderson, instead showing up in a plaid blazer. Turquoise and beige.

It was a postgame radio show done

After winning the NCAA national championship in 1996, Pitino and his wife, Joanne, finally relax and enjoy seven years of hard work — and reaching their dream.

courtside, with thousands of fans staying to listen.

It was the sideshows on the bench. Spike Lee and Muhammad Ali each sat on the UK bench for games. Actress Ashley Judd tried to sit. Couldn't keep still. Kept squirming, getting up on her knees, waving pom-pons as her beloved

Wildcats fans share their choice for President in 1996.

Cats rallied from a 22-point deficit at Vanderbilt's quirky old Memorial Gymnasium.

And, of course, Father Ed Bradley was a bench regular.

This was all a part of the Pitino package. The Catholic priest. The Runyonesque cast of Pitino cronies — guys with names like "Jersey Red" and "Johnny Joe Idaho."

Jersey Red was there in Italy when Pitino was ejected during an exhibition game loss in Montecatini. And when somone suggested that Pitino, who had been sitting down at the time, couldn't have possibly earned the ejection, Jersey responded with a knowing smile, "Oh, yes, he did."

It was the controversy over clothes. Not what Pitino wore, but what he had his team in. The shorts. The icicle ones. The too-close-to-Carolina-blue denim ones.

It was press conferences to assure would-be recruits that he was staying put.

It was watching the players — especially Rod Rhodes — running in and out of Pitino's doghouse.

It was Pitino in the 1997 NCAA Semifinal, hearing that Minnesota coach Clem Haskins had been whistled for a technical and instantly yelling "Derek!"

have a technical called on the other team.

But guess what? It all happened. And there was Anderson, flying off the bench to shoot the foul shot, giving the Wildcats a mental lift into what would prove to be Pitino's final game at UK a nail-biting, gut-turning, energy-sapping overtime loss to Arizona.

It was the way Pitino always was the

Tubby Smith (left) and Herb Sendek (middle) — both left Pitino's staff to become head coaches at other schools. Smith would return to Kentucky in 1997.

Ten weeks earlier, when leading scorer Derek Anderson had suffered the dreaded torn ACL, Pitino had promised to let him shoot a technical in the Final Four. At the time, it seemed like a far-fetched promise. First, UK had to make it to the Final Four without Anderson. Then it had to somehow

last one to walk out of the tunnel before a game. Head down. Almost like a fighter.

It was the time the Arkansas band waited for his entrance, broke into the theme from "The Godfather," causing Pitino's game-face to melt into a giant grin.

Pitino cuts down the net after the Wildcats defeated Auburn, 114-93, in 1991 and completed a season record of 22 wins and 6 losses. It would be their final year under NCAA probation.

It was the smile that crossed his face when midway through one game at Rupp Arena he looked over at a basket and saw that one of the ballboys — his youngest son, Ryan — had practically dozed off. "It was a slow game," he quipped afterward. "He's much quicker with a running style."

It was the Rick Pitino Care Center, Bravo Pitino, Pitino Pasta and The Pitino Signature Series Ford Explorer.

It was the hiring of Bernadette Locke-Mattox as the first female assistant in men's Division I basketball. And it was former trainer JoAnn Hauser suing UK, claiming she was a victim of sex discrimination and a "hostile working environment."

It was Pitino making a controversial appearance in Lexington with President Clinton on the eve of the 1996 election.

Republican U.S. Rep. Jim Bunning sent Pitino a telegram saying: "I just wanted you to know how disappointed and disgusted I was ... You definitely have lost ME as a UK fan.

Pitino fired back his own message: "I want YOU to know how disappointed and disgusted I was to receive your

Caption goes right here just like this. Caption goes right here just like this. Caption goes

telegram. ... If you would read the papers, you would see that I did not endorse Bill Clinton's candidacy. For your additional information, the president of the United States welcomed our team and my family and friends this year to the White House. It was attended by senators and congressmen ... I don't seem to recall you were present, so obviously whether you were a UK fan was in question to begin with."

It was the public opinion polls that showed Bunning had picked the wrong man to take on.

It was the Pitino Aura. The way he dressed, the way he walked, the way he handled pressure. Embraced it. Toyed with it. Savored it.

"That's what I love most about Kentucky," he said. "I think the pressure of Kentucky makes you work harder, focus better, play better defense, treat every game as if it's your last because it's so important to the people. And I think that's the fun part."

It was Pitino showing reverence for UK basketball, giving the players pregame pep talks about what it meant to walk onto a court with "KENTUCKY" on their chest.

It was Pitino showing irreverence for UK basketball, poking fun at the

Big Blue obsession.

Parents-to-be sent him sonograms of "future Wildcats." One woman called his radio show to tell him about the puppy she had just got. The dog was bright and energetic, she said, so she had decided to name him after her favorite coach: "Ricky P."

When he returned home from Philadelphia after getting beat by Laettner's shot and found out that someone had been going through his garbage, he said: "It's not what you'd call normal, but it's normal to Kentucky."

And when he had received an overnight letter from a doctor giving him some basketball tips before the trip to the Meadowlands with his soon-to-be national title team, Pitino had sent back a letter that said: "Thanks for your help. After the season I want to sit down with you and have a serious talk about how you're conducting surgery."

It was the players, starting with the most important recruit of his era, the one he got from New York: Jamal Mashburn.

It was the future NBA players who followed Mashburn: Antoine Walker, Tony Delk, Walter McCarty, Ron Mercer and Derek Anderson.

It was the Pitino assistants who left his side to become head coaches elsewhere: Tubby Smith, Herb Sendek, Billy Donovan, Ralph Willard.

It was three books in eight years.

It was going from a TV ban to making a record 12 appearances on ESPN in one season.

It was Pitino living up to his promise of putting Kentucky back on the cover of *Sports Illustrated*, only to find out that the cover proclaimed him: "A Man Possessed."

It was the nicknames he gave his teams. The Unforgettables. The Untouchables, The Unbelievables.

It was a lot of things. Most of all, though, it was fun.

When asked if he was concerned about Anderson and Mercer — The Air Pair — turning a fast break into a show, Pitino said: "That's like asking Pat Riley, 'Were you concerned about Magic and Worthy and those guys putting on a show?' That's what this is. It's entertainment."

It certainly was.

It ended with one last Pitino tradition: April Madness. The Lakers, the Nets, the Magic, the Warriors, the Sixers. It happened every spring. The NBA teams came calling.

Sixers owner Pat Croce told reporters in Philadelphia last spring:

"I'm going to love introducing Rick Pitino. I'm going to get him. I'm going to get him."

Croce, of course, didn't get him. It was the Celtics who made Pitino an offer he couldn't refuse. They not only opened the vault, they threw in an incentive: A storied franchise that had hit rock bottom and was looking for a savior to embrace.

So there he was nearly eight years after his arrival, saying goodbye, wearing a championship ring and a blue-and-white shirt.

"Kentucky," he said, "will always be in my heart."

Pitino shares strategy with his star pupil, Jamal Mashburn, during a break in the game against Vanderbilt in 1993.

Rodderick Rhodes (10) leaps for a rebound against LSU in 1993.

The Unforgettables: (top to bottom) John Pelphrey, Deron Feldhaus, Sean Woods and Richie Farmer.

Jamal Mashburn was selected as an all-American in 1993.

Tony Delk (00) stretches for a layup against Cagiva Varese, a professional basketball team from Italy, in 1995.

The acrobatic Jamal Mashburn reaches for a rebound against Morehead State in 1991.

*Antoine Walker
duels for the rebound
against Arkansas in
1996.*

Derek Anderson (23) taps in a basket against Vanderbilt in 1007.

Ron Mercer (33) fires a 3-point shot against
Syracuse in the 1996 NCAA championship game.

Antoine Walker (24) and Walter McCarty (40) corralled Tim Duncan in their meeting in the 1996 Midwest Regionals.

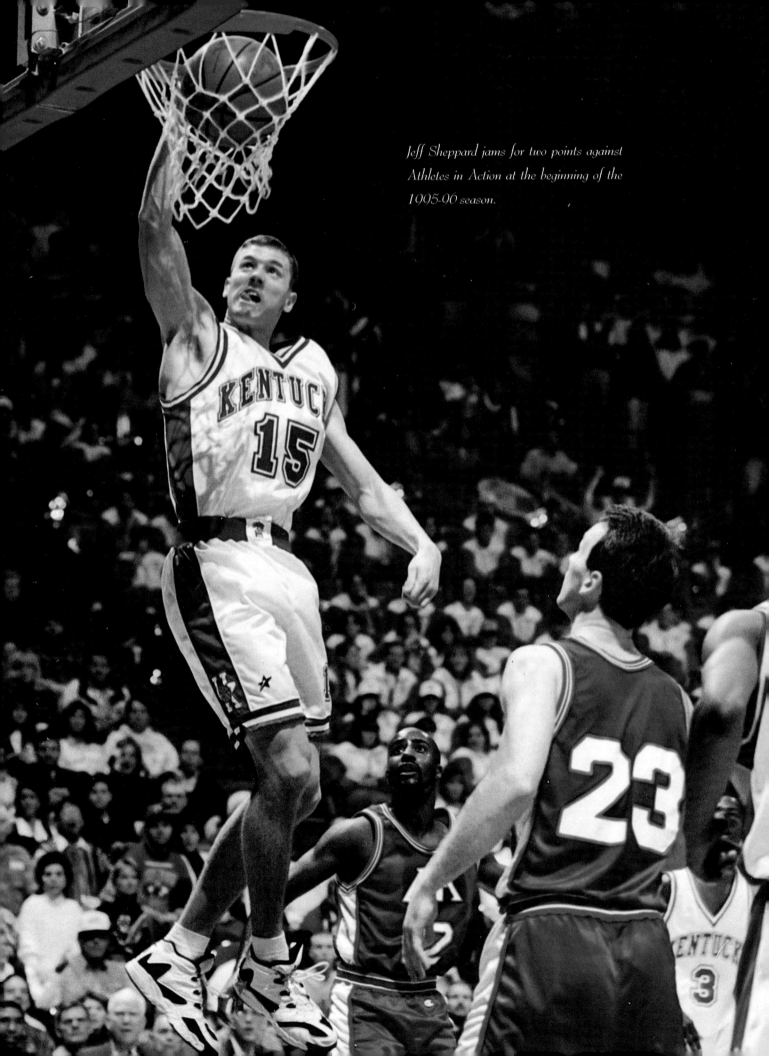

Jeff Sheppard jams for two points against
Athletes in Action at the beginning of the
1995-96 season.

Wildcats athletic director C.M. Newton and Pitino rebuilt Kentucky into the "Roman Empire," which put Walter McCarty (40), Tony Delk (00) and their teammates on top of the college basketball world.

The Wildcats celebrate their sixth national championship after defeating Syracuse in the 1996 NCAA championship game.

Left: Walter McCarty (40) steals the rebound from UMass' Marcus Camby in the 1996 Final Four.

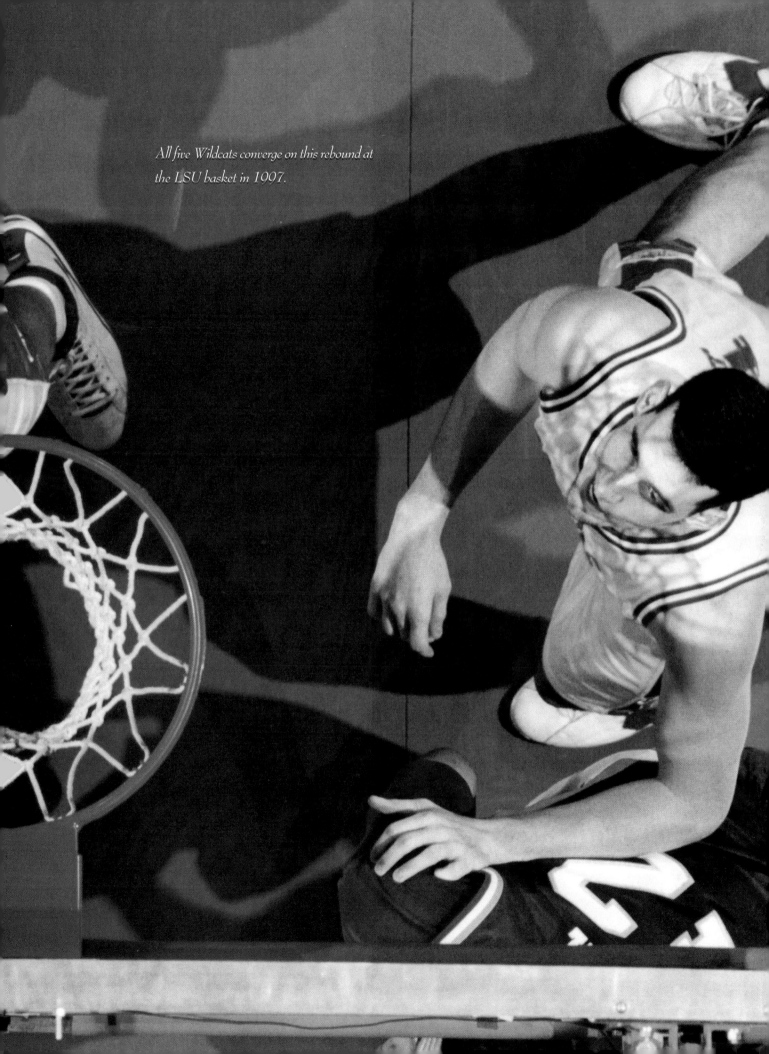

All five Wildcats converge on this rebound at
the LSU basket in 1997.

Anthony Epps races past a Syracuse defender in the 1996 NCAA championship game.

Right: Walter McCarty's memorable basket against UMass sealed the Wildcats' 81-74 victory in the 1996 Final Four.

Derek Anderson at the free throw line shooting technical free throws against Minnesota in the 1997 NCAA Final Four. Anderson is the only player in Final Four history to score with no actual playing time.

Tony Delk (00) races upcourt against Arkansas in the 1996 SEC Tournament.

Pitino takes his turn in cutting down the net after the Wildcats defeated Syracuse, 76-67, in the 1996 NCAA championship game.

Right: Wayne Turner glides for an easy layup against Arizona in the 1997 NCAA championship game, which Arizona won in overtime.

Kentucky Wildcats Basketball Lettermen

A

Allan Abramson	(Mgr.) (44)
John Adams	(63, 64, 65)
Don Adkins	(63 64, 65)
Earl Adkins	(55, 57, 58)
Paul Adkins	(21, 22)
Marvin Akers	(41, 42, 43)
Charles Alberts	(25, 26)
Charles Aleksinas	(78)
Ermal Allen	(40, 41, 42)
Ed Allin	(45)
Sean Alteri (Mgr.)	(97)
Carl Althaus	(43)
H.M. Amoss	(04)
Derek Anderson	(96, 97)
Dwight Anderson	(79)
Milerd Anderson	(34,35,36)
Jim Andrews	(71, 72, 73)
Paul Andrews	(84, 85, 86, 87)
Lee Andrus	(03, 04)
Phil Argento	(67, 68, 69)
R.H. Arnett	(04)
Jay Atkerson	(Mgr.) (57, 58, 59)
Randy Azbill	(Mgr.) (84, 85)

B

H.A. Babb	(Mgr.) (11)
Adrian Back	(42)
Stanley Baer	(05, 06, 07)
Scotty Baesler	(62, 63)
Mike Ballenger	(82)
R.C. Barbee	(06, 07, 09)
Cliff Barker	(47, 48, 49)
Bill Barlow	(43)
B. Barnett	(11, 12, 13)
Dale Barnstable	(47, 48, 49, 50)
Bobby Barton	(Mgr.) (67)

Arthur Bash	(18)
Dickey Beal	(81, 82, 83, 84)
Ralph Beard	(46, 47, 48, 49)
Bret Bearup	(81, 83, 84, 85)
Todd Bearup	(91)
Ed Beck	(56, 57, 58)
Cecil Bell	(31)
Winston Bennett	(84, 85, 86, 88)
Cliff Berger	(66, 67, 68)
Henry Besuden	(26)
Bill Bibb	(54)
Arthur Bicknell	(40)
Doug Billips	(Mgr.) (69, 70)
Jerry Bird	(54, 55, 56)
James Blackmon	(84, 85, 86, 87)
Crittenden Blair	(34)
Harry Bliss	(35)
Dave Bolen	(Mgr.) (96, 97)
Ralph Boren	(24)
Brad Bounds	(66, 67)
Sam Bowie	(80, 81, 84)
Junior Braddy	(90, 91, 92, 93)
Bob Brannum	(44, 47)
Jeff Brassow	(90, 91, 93, 94)
D.P. Branson	(05, 06)
Wayne Breeden	(Mgr.) (83)
John Brewer	(55, 56, 57)
Leo Brewer	(08)
Melvin Brewer	(41, 42, 43)
G.C. Bridges	(10)
Jake Bronston	(30, 31)
Dale Brown	(92, 93)
Steve Bruce	(87)
T.R. Bryant	(05, 06, 07)
Nathanial Buis	(44)
Carey Burchett	(Mgr.) (34)
Carroll Burchett	(60, 61, 62)
L.S. Burhham	(19, 20, 22,23)

Bob Burrow (55, 56)
Bill Busey (68)
Kirk Byars (Mgr.) (63)
Leroy Byrd (84, 85, 86)

C

Gerry Calvert (55, 56, 57)
George Campbell (Mgr.) (35)
Kenton Campbell (45, 46)
Patrick Campbell (17, 18)
Burgess Carey (25, 26)
Ralph Carlisle (35, 36, 37)
Armiel Carman (Mgr.) (16)
Dwane Casey (76, 77, 78, 79)
Mike Casey (68, 69, 71)
Billy Ray Cassady (56, 57, 58)
J.S. Chambers (Mgr.) (09)
Rex Chapman (87, 88)
Truman Claytor (76, 77, 78, 79)
Steve Clevenger (66, 67, 68)
Marion Cluggish (38, 39, 40)
Bernie Coffman (59, 60)
Sid Cohen (59, 60)
L. Collinsworth (56, 57, 58)
Carl Combs (40)
Cecil Combs (28, 29, 30)
Charles Combs (38)
Larry Conley (64, 65, 66)
Jimmy Dan Conner (73, 74, 75)
Joe Coons (05)
Anthony Cooper (90)
Fred Cowan (78, 79, 80, 81)
Johnny Cox (57, 58, 59)
Hugh Coy (54)
John Crigler (56, 57, 58)
George Critz (64)
Larry Crosby (Mgr.) (65)
John S. Crosthwaite (10)

Albert Cummins (47)
Fred Curtis (37, 38, 39)

D

Louie Dampier (65, 66, 67)
Darrell Darby (31, 32, 33)
Howard Dardeen (59)
Ed Davender (85, 86, 87, 88)
Berkley Davis (34)
Bruce Davis (36)
Johnathon Davis (89, 90, 91)
Mulford Davis (43, 46, 47)
Robert Davis (37)
William Davis (33, 34)
David Deaton (Mgr.) (89)
Ted Deeken (62, 63, 64)
Claire Dees (27, 28, 29)
Tony Delk (93, 94, 95, 96)
John "Frenchy" DeMoisey
(32, 33, 34)
Truitt DeMoisey (34)
Harry Denham (39)
Rodney Dent (93, 94)
Jim Dinwiddie (69, 70, 71)
J.A. Dishman (18, 19)
A.L. Dolan (06)
Mike Dolan (Mgr.) (52, 54)
Warfield Donohue (35, 36, 37)
H.H. Downing (08)
Pat Doyle (63)
Rick Drewitz (72, 73, 74)
Hunter Durham (Mgr.) (61, 62)
James Durham (45)

E

Ray Edelman (72, 73, 74)
Allen Edwards (95, 96, 97)
Leroy Edwards (35)

Russell Ellington	(35, 36)
LeRon Ellis	(88. 89)
Randy Embry	(63, 64, 65)
Kenneth England	(41, 42)
Anthony Epps	(94, 95, 96, 97)
Bill Evans	(52, 54, 55)
William Evans	(Mgr.) (42)
J.C. Everett	(19, 20)

F

H.L. Farmer	(12, 13)
Richie Farmer	(89, 90, 91, 92)
Keith Farnsely	(39, 40, 41)
John Farris	(Mgr.) (92, 94, 95)
J.B. Faulconer	(Mgr.) (39)
Allen Feldhaus	(60, 61, 62)
Deron Feldhaus	(89, 90, 91, 92)
John Ferguson	(Mgr.) (71)
Fred Fest	(23)
Garrett Fitzpatrick	(Mgr.) (41)
George Fletcher	(Mgr.) (80, 81)
Chigger Flynn	(Mgr.) (56)
Mike Flynn	(73, 74, 75)
Bob Fowler	(76)
Travis Ford	(92, 93, 94)
W.C. Fox	(07, 08, 09)

G

J.H. Gaiser	(10, 11, 12)
Gary Gamble	(66, 67, 68)
Kenneth Gayheart	(Mgr.) (90, 91, 92, 94)
Robert Gayheart	(Mgr.) (89)
Chris Gettelfinger	(80, 81)
Elmer Gilb	(29)
Jeff Ginnan	(89)
Jack Givens	(75, 76, 77, 78)
Max Glickman	(18)

James Goforth	(35, 36, 37)
Zach Goins	(Mgr.) (97)
James Goodman	(38, 39)
Phil Grawemeyer	(54, 55, 56)
Sean Gray	(Mgr.) (94, 95, 96, 97)
Kevin Grevey	(73, 74, 75)
William Griffeth	(Mgr.) (29)
Alex Groza	(45, 47, 48, 49)
George Gumbert	(14, 15, 16)
Bob Guyette	(73, 74, 75)
J. White Guyn	(04)

H

Cliff Hagan	(51, 52, 54)
Joseph Hagan	(36, 37, 38)
Jerry Hale	(73, 74, 75)
Dan Hall	(75)
Reggie Hanson	(88, 89, 90, 91)
Roger Harden	(83, 84, 85, 86)
Philip Haring	(Mgr.) (36, 38)
Sam Harper	(63, 64)
Tom Harper	(64)
Carson Harreld	(Mgr.) (65, 66)
Chris Harrison	(92, 93, 94, 95)
W.C. Harrison	(11, 12)
D.W. Hart	(11, 12, 16)
Merion Haskins	(75, 76, 77)
Vernon Hatton	(56, 57, 58)
Basil Hayden	(20, 21, 22)
Elmo Head	(37, 38, 39)
Tom Heitz	(80, 82, 83, 84)
G. Foster Helm	(25, 27)
J.H. Herman	(06)
Walter Hirsch	(49, 51)
Walter Hodge	(37)
Joe Holland	(46, 47, 48)
Joey Holland	(76)
Kent Hollenbeck	(70, 71, 72)

Derrick Hord	(80, 81, 82, 83)
Mike Howard	(Mgr.) (96, 97)
Dick Howe	(57, 58)
Lee Huber	(39, 40, 41)
C.T. Hughes	(24, 25)
Lowell Hughes	(58, 59)
Harry Hurd	(62)
Charles Hurt	(80, 81, 82, 83)

I

R.Y. Ireland	(16, 17)
Charles Ishmael	(63, 64)
Dan Issel	(68, 69, 70)

J

Ralph Jackowski	(38)
Thad Jaracz	(66, 67, 68)
Irvine Jeffries	(28)
Cedric Jenkins	(85, 86, 87, 88)
Paul Jenkins	(26, 27, 28)
Ned Jennings	(59, 60, 61)
Herbert Jerome	(34)
Ellis Johnson	(31, 32, 33)
Larry Johnson	(74, 75, 76, 77)
Phil Johnson	(56, 58, 59)
Walter Johnson	(44)
Chris Jones	(89)
Wallace Jones	(46, 47, 48, 49)
James Jordan	(47, 48)

K

Pat Kelly	(05)
William P. Kemper	(Mgr.) (05)
Ron Kennett	(64)
Stan Key	(70, 71, 72)
Jeff Kidder	(Mgr.) (89)
James King	(40, 41, 42)
William King	(21, 22, 24)

A.M. Kirby	(07)
William Kleiser	(32)
Edwin Knadler	(27)
Howard Kreuter	(32, 33)
Tommy Kron	(64, 65, 66)

L

Art Laib	(68)
Ed Lander	(42, 43)
Bo Lanter	(80, 81, 82)
Phil Latham	(Trn.) (74, 75)
Jason Lathrem	(96)
Bob Lavin	(20, 21, 22)
Dave Lawrence	(33, 34, 35)
Roger Layne	(51)
James Lee	(75, 76, 77, 78)
Ken Lehkamp	(Mgr.) (56, 57)
Jim LeMaster	(66, 67, 68)
Larry Lentz	(66)
Morris Levin	(Mgr.) (31)
Garland Lewis	(34, 35, 36)
Billy Ray Lickert	(59, 60, 61)
James Line	(47, 48, 49, 50)
Shelby Linville	(50, 51, 52)
Ercel Little	(32)
Steve Lochmueller	(73, 74)
Robert Lock	(85, 86, 87, 88)
Dutch Longworth	(17)
Ronnie Lyons	(72, 73, 74)

M

Kyle Macy	(78, 79, 80)
Richard Madison	(85, 86, 87, 88)
Jamaal Magloire	(97)
Eric Manual	(88)
F.L. Marx	(10, 11)
B.G. Marsh	(18)
Gimel Martinez	(91, 92, 93, 94)

Jamal Mashburn	(91, 92, 93)
Steve Masiello	(97)
Jim Master	(81, 82, 83, 84)
James Mathewson	(42)
Charles Maxson	(Mgr.) (33)
Jack May	(Mgr.) (35, 36)
John McAdam	(Mgr.) (70)
Walter McCarty	(94, 95, 96)
Paul McBrayer	(28, 29, 30)
Bob McCowan	(69, 72)
Jim McDonald	(60, 61, 62)
James McFarland	(24, 25, 26)
Skip McGaw	(90)
Lawrence McGinnis	(28, 29, 30)
Louis McGinnis	(29, 30, 31)
James McIntosh	(37)
Troy McKinley	(82, 83, 84, 85)
J. McKinney	(Mgr.) (36, 37)
C.F. Meadors	(12)
Ron Mercer	(96, 97)
Hub Metry	(Mgr.) (64, 65)
Derrick Miller	(87, 88, 89, 90)
Cameron Mills	(95, 96, 97)
Chris Mills	(89)
Don Mills	(58, 59, 60)
Ray Mills	(55, 56, 57)
Terry Mills	(69, 70, 71)
Stanley Milward	(28, 29, 30)
Will Milward	(24, 25)
Dirk Minniefield	(80, 81, 82, 83)
Terry Mobley	(63, 64, 65)
Nazr Mohammed	(96, 97)
Gayle Mohney	(26)
Bob Moore	(Mgr.) (50, 51, 52)
Eric Moore	(Mgr.) (89)
Ralph Morgan	(13, 14, 15)
Jeff Morrow	(Mgr.) (89, 90, 91, 92)
Tom Moseley	(44)

N

Cotton Nash	(62, 63, 64)
Alonzo Nelson	(45)
Roger Newman	(61)
C.M. Newton	(51)
Tommy Nichols	(36)
Paul Noel	(43)
Randy Noll	(70)

O

Dan Omlor	(Mgr.) (64)
Bernard Opper	(37, 38, 39)
Hays Owens	(28, 29, 30)

P

Scott Padgett	(95, 97)
Harold Park	(Mgr.) (45)
James Park	(14)
Michael Parks	(90)
Clyde Parker	(43)
Ed Parker	(Mgr.) (19)
J. Ed Parker	(45, 46, 47)
Tom Parker	(70, 71, 72)
Jack Parkinson	(44, 45, 46, 48)
Dick Parsons	(59, 60, 61)
Tom Payne	(71)
Bart Peak	(17)
Leonard Pearson	(50)
John Pelphrey	(89, 90, 91, 92)
Doug Pendygraft	(62)
E.S. Penick	(43)
Dan Perry	(72)
George Perry	(Mgr.)(54)
Mike Phillips	(75, 76, 77, 78)
Frank Phipps	(27)
Wayne Plummer	(09)
Randy Pool	(68, 69)
Mark Pope	(95, 96)

Tommy Porter	(66, 67, 68)
Shelby Post	(08, 09)
Sam Potter	(34)
William Poynz	(21, 23)
Mike Pratt	(68, 69, 70)
R.C. Preston	(11, 12, 13, 14)
Jared Prickett	(93, 94, 95, 97)
Linville Puckett	(54)
Larry Pursiful	(60, 61, 62)

R

Frank Ramsey	(51, 52, 54)
Lloyd Ramsey	(41, 42)
Tripp Ramsey	(Mgr.) (76, 77)
Robert Reynolds	(32)
Rodrick Rhodes	(93, 94, 95)
A.T. Rice	(23, 24)
S.H. Ridgeway	(20, 21)
Andre Riddick	(92, 93, 94, 95)
Carl Riefkin	(23, 24)
Pat Riley	(65, 66, 67)
R.N. Roark	(04)
Roy Roberts	(62, 63)
Rick Robey	(75, 76, 77, 78)
Al Robinson	(59)
William "Doc" Rodes	(17)
William Rodes	(09, 10)
Karl Rohs	(25)
Don Rolfes	(63)
Kenneth Rollins	(43, 47, 48)
Van Buren Ropke	(27)
Gayle Rose	(52, 54, 55)
Harold Ross	(56, 57, 58)
Ben Roth	(Mgr.) (15)
Layton Rouse	(38, 39, 40)
Willie Rouse	(54)
Tony Russell	(Mgr.) (94, 95, 96, 97)
Herky Rupp	(61)

S

Forest Sale	(31, 32, 33)
Charles Schrader	(14, 17)
Wilber Schu	(44, 45, 46)
Herschel Scott	(13, 14, 15)
Mike Scott	(87, 88, 89)
Jim Server	(15, 16)
Evan Settle	(33, 34)
A.P. Shanklin	(18)
Shelby Shanklin	(08)
James Sharpe	(27)
Jeff Sheppard	(94, 95, 96)
Jay Shidler	(77, 78, 79, 80)
Terry Shigg	(87)
Oliver Simmons	(96)
Glenn Sims	(Mgr.) (73)
George Skinner	(33)
Bobby Slusher	(59)
Adrian Smith	(57, 58)
Bill Smith	(56, 57, 58)
G.J. Smith	(73, 74, 75)
G.K. Smith	(21, 23)
Mark Soderberg	(70)
Carey Spicer	(29, 30, 31)
Bill Spivey	(50, 51)
Vincent Splane	(42)
Carl Staker	(40, 41, 42)
Larry Stamper	(71, 72, 73)
Larry Steele	(69, 70, 71)
Tim Stephens	(77, 78)
Gene Stewart	(67)
Bobby Stilz	(67)
C.P. St. John	(04)
Brian Stocker	(Mgr.) (94, 95, 96, 97)
N. Stone	(08)
John Strogh	(45, 48)
Guy Strong	(50)

William Sturgill	(45, 46)
Todd Svoboda	(93)
Don Sullivan	(Mgr.) (78, 79)
Bill Surface	(Mgr.) (55)
Sean Sutton	(88, 89)

T

Bob Tallent	(66)
Spencer Tatum	(Mgr.) (89, 90, 91, 92)
Vincent Tatum	(Mgr.) (91, 92)
Bob Taylor	(35)
Alan Theobald	(Mgr.) (68)
H.C. Thomas	(18, 19)
Henry Thomas	(91, 92)
Irving Thomas	(86, 87)
Roger Thomas	(Mgr.) (82, 83)
Homer Thompson	(37, 38, 39)
Tommy Thompson	(Mgr.) (60)
Milton Ticco	(41, 42, 43)
E.J. Tierney	(35)
Clarence Tillman	(79)
Aminu Timberlake	(92, 93)
Jack Tingle	(44, 45, 46, 47)
Carlos Toomer	(91, 92)
Garland Townes	(50)
Bill Trott	(31)
Lou Tsioropoulos	(51, 52, 54)
Jack Tucker	(33, 34, 35)
Wayne Turner	(96, 97)
Melvin Turpin	(81, 82, 83, 84)
Paul Turrell	(35)
William P. Tuttle	(12, 13, 14 15)

U

Eiki Umezaki	(Mgr.) (89)
Lovell Underwood	(24, 25, 26)

V

Arthur Vastin	(18)
Chuck Verderber	(79, 80, 81, 82)
Frank Vogel	(Mgr.) (96)
George Vulich	(44, 45)

W

Antoine Walker	(95, 96)
J. Rice Walker	(36, 37, 38)
Kenny Walker	(83, 84, 85, 86)
Reggie Warford	(76)
L.B. Waters	(05)
Robert Watson	(50, 51, 52)
A.J. Weisenberger	(11, 13)
Wylie B. Wendt	(06)
Leo Wenkley	(Mgr.) (30)
Clint Wheeler	(71)
Lucian Whitaker	(50, 51, 52)
Waller White	(40, 41, 42)
Don Whitehead	(44)
E. Wiheling	(21)
W.G. Wilkinson	(23)
LaVon Williams	(77, 78, 79, 80)
Maury Wilson	(06, 07, 08)
W.C. Wilson	(13)
Phil Whitt	(Trn.) (77)
Sean Woods	(90, 91, 92)
Charles Worthington	(31, 32)
H.J. Wurtele	(04)

Y

George Yates	(30, 31, 33)
H. Yessin	(Mgr.) (46, 47, 48, 49)
Rudy Yessin	(44)

Z

George Zerfoss	(16, 18)
Karl Zerfoss	(13, 15, 16)
Tom Zerfoss	(14)
Todd Ziegler	(85, 86)

Photo Credits

Bettman Archives: 38, 63, 64-65, 66, 68, 131.

CBS-TV: 172.

David Coyle: Front Cover, 33, 35, 112, 136, 143, 144, 146, 147, 149, 150, 153, 154, 158, 161, 163, 164-165, 168, 169, 171, 177, 178, 179, 181, 182-183.

The Courier-Journal: 13, 20, 29, 36, 42-43, 48, 53, 56-57, 76, 102, 104-105, 106, 109, 121, 122, 123, 124, 125, 126, 130, 132, 133, 139, 160, 162.

Helena Hav: 174-175.

NCAA Photos: Back Cover, 34, 90-91, 113, 114-115, 116, 118-119, 166-167, 173, 176, 180.

University of Kentucky: 4, 6, 7, 8-both, 11, 12, 13, 14, 15-both, 16, 17, 18-19, 20-21, 22-23, 24, 26-27, 28, 30, 31, 40-41, 44, 58-both, 59, 60-61, 62-both, 64-both, 67, 69, 72-73, 74-both, 75, 77, 78, 79, 80, 81, 82, 83, 84-85, 86-87, 88, 89, 92-93, 94, 95-both, 96, 98, 100-101, 111, 117, 120, 127, 128, 134, 135, 140-141, 148, 151, 152, 157, 159, 170.

Wide World Photo: 10-11, 70-71, 129.